Notable or Notorious?

Notable or Notorious?
A Gallery of Parisians

Gordon Wright

Harvard University Press
Cambridge, Massachusetts
London, England
1991

The last, like the first,
for Louise
Companion and Critic

First Harvard University Press paperback edition, 1991

This edition published by arrangement with The Portable Stanford

Library of Congress Cataloging-in-Publication Data

Wright, Gordon, 1912–
    Notable or notorious? : a gallery of Parisians / Gordon Wright.
        p.   cm.
    Reprint. Originally published: Stanford, Calif. : Stanford Alumni
Association, © 1989. (The Portable Stanford)
    ISBN 0-674-62743-1
    1. Paris (France)—Biography.   2. Paris (France)—Intellectual
life—19th century.   3. Paris (France)—Social life and
customs—19th century.   I. Title.
DC705.A1W75   1991
994'.3606'0922—dc20   90-47629
[B]   CIP

Cover Art: Gustave Caillebotte, *A Rainy Day*
(Intersection of the Rue de Turin and Rue de Moscou),
1877, oil on canvas, 212.2 × 276.2
Charles H. and Mary F. S. Worcester Fund,
© 1989 The Art Institute of Chicago.
All rights reserved.

Contents

Credits

Introduction

On the Seine's left bank in the heart of Paris, an imposing new museum opened its doors in 1986. The Musée d'Orsay, housed in a massive turn-of-the-century structure that had once been a railway station, was designed to celebrate the cultural glories of France in the nineteenth century. Since opening day, throngs of visitors have crowded its galleries; already it has become one of the city's proudest monuments.

The museum offers us a new opportunity to evaluate and appreciate a period that has often been disparaged as dull, meretricious, or simply bourgeois. "The Stupid Nineteenth Century" the journalist Léon Daudet called it in one of his typical diatribes. Yet it is not easy to suggest another century, save perhaps the seventeenth, in which Paris produced such a galaxy of stars: artists, writers, composers, thinkers. True, the galaxy shines less brightly in the firmaments of politics and economics—though even here, posterity may have been too negative. In retrospect, some politicians begin to take on the qualities of statesmen, and the business-industrial élite appears less benighted than it was once judged to be. At any rate, the d'Orsay provides a stunning showcase for the artistic segment of the century's constellation of talent; it has already inspired a revived interest in the period's creative energies as a whole.

One striking facet of the museum's collection is that alongside the works of art long recognized as masterpieces, the visitor finds scores of paintings and sculptures newly resurrected from obscure storerooms. For the most part, their long exile is understandable; somehow they lack the spark of genius. Yet their emergence from limbo enables us to view the nineteenth century in the round, as men and women of the time experienced it. We can compare the tastes and values of that period with those of our own time, and can see more clearly why many former luminaries have lost their luster. At the same time, their resurrection may in the end restore a few of these forgotten artists to the recognition they deserve.

This book, save for one chapter, is not concerned with artists. It is concerned with men and women who achieved a degree of prominence or notoriety in the Paris of their day, but whose reputations have been dimmed by time. While they are not "world-historical" figures in the Hegelian sense, each one seems to me to reflect some aspect of the society and attitudes of nineteenth-century Parisians. Indeed, they may be even more representative of their times than are the certified geniuses, those whose stature makes them exceptional rather than typical.

That is one reason why I have chosen to write about a series of these Parisians. Their lives, loosely linked together in a sequence that runs through the whole nineteenth century, may provide entry points for an understanding of that complex and self-centered world, with its distinct but overlapping circles of élites. I may as well confess, however, to a more subjective reason for choosing these characters rather than others: namely, old-fashioned curiosity. Over the years, their names have turned up from time to time in the course of my reading, though in most cases I was only vaguely informed about their lives. Curiosity may not be the best motive for the historian; indeed, Gibbon's pithy advice to an aspiring young scholar was "never pursue the curious." Yet curiosity can lead one not only into byways and dead ends, as Gibbon suggested, but also into new paths to understanding. And if one believes that history is about men and women as well as about trends, underlying forces, statistical categories, and disembodied ideas, curiosity can dredge up some intriguing characters and some piquant episodes out of the past.

Midway through the nineteenth century the prominent journalist Villemessant issued the following pronouncement, salted no doubt with a touch of irony: "A dog that drowns in Paris is more interesting than a world that collapses elsewhere." Outrageous hyperbole, of course; yet for those who have been extensively exposed to the charms of that city, an understandable sentiment.

NOUVEAU PARIS MONUMENTAL

ITINÉRAIRE PRATIQUE DE L'ÉTRANGER DANS PARIS

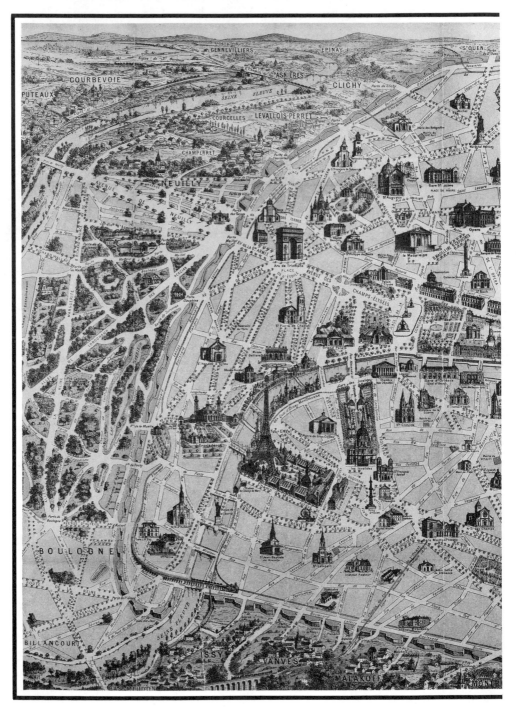

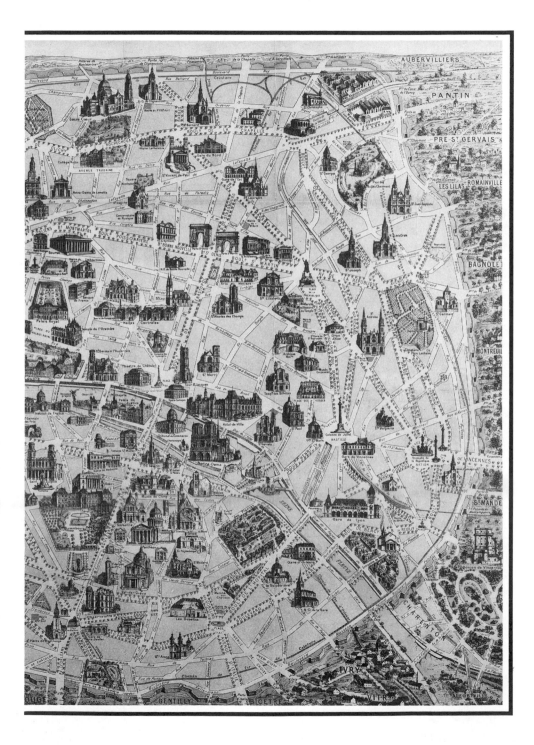

Imp. d'Aubert & Cᵉ

1839 587

M︤ᵐᵉ︥ EMILE DE GIRARDIN,

Née Delphine Gay.

1

Delphine Gay
Princess of the Salons

Paris in the early decades of the nineteenth century was a favorite hunting ground for opportunists. The Great Revolution had, like an earthquake, shaken France's social foundations; ambitious men and women, if they were lucky and clever, could rise faster and higher than ever before. Stendhal, in *The Red and the Black*, has given us the prototype of such social climbers, although his hero Julien Sorel ended tragically. In some ways Delphine Gay can be seen as Julien's feminine equivalent. As a woman in a male-dominated society, she found more serious obstacles than Julien; but in the end she surmounted them more successfully.

Delphine enjoyed some initial advantages: she was relatively well-born; her father, through connections, had been appointed by Napoleon's government to the lucrative post of tax collector in one of the newly annexed Rhineland provinces. Delphine was born there, in Aix-la-Chapelle, in 1804, and was named for the heroine of Madame de Stael's best-selling novel *Delphine*. Her mother, Sophie Gay, enjoyed a modest reputation in Paris as an author of novels and plays. But Sophie also had an active and wicked tongue, and in-

1

dulged it once too often at the expense of her husband's bureaucratic chief. Gay *père*, dismissed from his post in 1808, stayed on in the Rhineland in an effort to establish a bank, while Sophie and her child returned to Paris. There, moving from one cramped apartment to another, they managed to survive through Sophie's indefatigable writing; she even managed to mount a literary salon that attracted a coterie of notables—the painters Vernet and Gros, the writers Benjamin Constant, Chateaubriand and Latouche, and the brilliant tragedian Talma.

From earliest childhood, this was Delphine's world. Salon society was her natural habitat, and it remained her milieu throughout her life. At age sixteen she was introduced as a full participant in her mother's salon, where she soon became its star attraction. A statuesque blonde beauty, tactful and gracious, she inherited her mother's wit without its malicious edge. Besides, she showed precocious literary talent; at age eighteen she entered the Académie Française's poetry competition, and was awarded a special prize that made her an instant celebrity. Hailed as the *"muse de la patrie,"* she received (on her mother's urgent appeal) a royal grant of 800 francs annually and an audience with King Charles X. Her poetry was classical enough to please conservative tastes, but she also found admirers among the rising young romantics, some of whom were welcomed at Sophie's salon. On the celebrated occasion in 1830 when Victor Hugo's *Hernani* provoked a riotous confrontation between romantics and classicists at the Théâtre-Français, the romantics in the audience turned to Delphine as she entered her box and saluted her with a triple round of applause. But she lost her state pension when an incautious witticism in one of her poems infuriated the king. The Gay household was once more reduced to respectable penury.

The obvious solution was of course an advantageous marriage. For some time, Sophie had been on the lookout for a suitable match for her handsome and talented daughter. At one point the young poet Alfred de Vigny had been the favored choice, but Vigny's class-conscious mother vetoed that arrangement even though it seems to have been a love match. Several other candidates crossed the horizon, but one after another faded from view—in part because Delphine could provide no dowry, but also because suitors were scared off by the prospect of the domineering Sophie as mother-in-law. For a time, before she lost Charles X's favor, there was talk in court circles of a possible romantic liaison with the widower-king. Fortunately for Delphine, it remained mere talk. In 1826, mother and daughter sought greener fields in Italy, where they stayed for more than a year. Delphine was received there as a visiting celebrity; she won the warm admiration of the young French diplomat-poet Alphonse de Lamartine, and was briefly affianced to an Italian aristocrat. Back in Paris in 1827 still without a husband, Delphine and Sophie sensed that time was beginning to press; at twenty-three, the threat of spinsterhood loomed up ahead. Yet four more years were to go by before a satisfactory match could at last be arranged. In 1831, at the age of twenty-seven, she married a man two years her junior—a man of somewhat obscure origins and of still uncertain future, Emile de Girardin.

For some time Girardin had been an assiduous but rather shadowy presence at the Gay salon, where he always managed to sit close to Delphine in an attitude of silent worship. Even more than Delphine, he bore the Julien Sorel mark. Born of the extramarital amours of a Napoleonic army officer, Alexandre de Girardin, he was falsely registered at birth as Emile Delamothe and was relegated to foster homes in Paris and Normandy. At age eighteen he returned to Paris to seek fame and fortune, both of which eluded him for some years. He haunted the boulevards and the smart cafés, ventured briefly into a couple of professional careers, then tried his luck as a writer with only mediocre success. Finally, in 1828, he hit upon his true calling as a press entrepreneur. He created one after another a series of specialized magazines, to one of which both Sophie and Delphine were invited to contribute. Within a decade he was to become the Rupert Murdoch of his day, and would glory in the label "the Napoleon of the press."

When Delphine married him in 1831, however, his real triumphs were still ahead. Did her acceptance of Girardin rest on a shrewd assessment of his potential? If so, she had a remarkable flair as talent-spotter, for until then Girardin had displayed more ambition and energy than true genius. Perhaps, as other prospects faded, she had grown desperate. Or possibly some indefinable attraction initially brought the couple together, though an introverted loner like Girardin was hardly the sort to inflame the sentiments of a young social beauty. Reading backward from their quarter-century of married life, one is inclined to see the match as the product of mutual opportunism. Girardin clearly had something to gain by their union: access to a social circle of some distinction, and to the group of talented writers who frequented the Gay salon. Delphine's calculations involved more risk; but if Girardin's star were to rise, she could hope for a share of his glory and a life of comfort, perhaps even opulence.

Whether or not conjugal affection marked the first years of their marriage, such tender sentiments were not to last long. For one thing, Girardin was by nature a workaholic; he begrudged any time wasted in what he regarded as frivolous pursuits. Avid for wealth and power, each of his triumphs only whetted his appetite for more. In 1834 he won a seat in Parliament, and he remained a deputy (with one interruption) until 1848. His political talents, however, were unimpressive; he hated public speaking, rarely rose to the rostrum, and harbored an ill-concealed contempt for most politicians. His influence came rather from his role as press tycoon and editorialist. In 1836 he launched France's first mass circulation daily, *La Presse*, which quickly achieved a smashing success. His forceful editorials soon made him a power in the land; his support of King Louis-Philippe's regime was marked by a spirit of critical independence.

Girardin's single-minded pursuit of status and power left Delphine free to shape her own life. She naturally chose to continue writing, turning more and more from poetry to prose, and to establish her own salon. As Girardin's prosperity increased, the couple moved steadily upscale—first to 11 rue Saint-Georges, in a quarter undergoing gentrification, and eventually to a mansion just off the Champs-Elysées. As a salon hostess Delphine succeeded brilliantly; indeed, Sophie complained that many of her faithful acolytes had deserted the mother for the daughter. Delphine's beauty, wit, and charm, her warmth of personality, attracted the literary élite of Paris: Victor Hugo, Lamartine, Eugène Sue, Théophile Gautier became habitués. These literary lions were joined by some prominent politicians also— Thiers for a time, then his rival Guizot—along with other supporters of the bourgeois monarchy. Girardin dropped in occasionally, but rarely participated in the talk; more often he sat quietly in a corner, dozed off, or slipped out to his study. But Delphine's salon served him well, for it gave him social status and provided him with a stable of literary contributors to *La Presse*. Among Girardin's specialties was the feuilleton, a long-running serial novel carried daily on the front page, with impressive results for the paper's circulation figures. Girardin raised the feuilleton to new heights by recruiting such stars as Balzac, Sue, and Alexandre Dumas.

Was Delphine satisfied with her active but loveless role in this marriage? There is no reason to suppose that she was not content. Girardin provided the resources for the most successful Paris salon of the day and the leisure to pursue her own literary career. She in turn provided him with the social relationships that he found useful but was temperamentally incapable of developing on his own. If Delphine allowed herself to be used for her husband's purposes, she saw nothing wrong in that. She admired Girardin, shone in his reflected glory, deferred to him as master of the household. If she was wounded by his cold indifference, she gave no outward sign of it. Indeed, she made no complaint when Girardin turned to philandering, indulged in a series of ill-concealed love affairs, including one with the notorious courtesan Esther Guimont, and even produced an illegitimate son. Instead, she took in the love child and adopted him as her own.

Viewed in the light of today's American mores, such circumstances may make Delphine seem a pathetic victim and a model of feminine self-sacrifice. Possibly she was; but it is more likely that she saw her relationship with Girardin as quite normal. Countess Marie d'Agoult, like Delphine a writer and a noted salon hostess, has given us in her memoirs an unvarnished description of the tribal customs of Parisian high society in her times. "In aristocratic circles," she wrote, "the husband as husband counted for very little. After a very short time, a man who devoted himself to his wife would have seemed ridiculous. To be seen constantly at her side, either at home or in the salons, would have earned him a reputation as a fool or a bore. Soon after marriage, a wife was glad to see her husband find someplace else to spend his time. Any *'galant homme'*, to avoid being at loose ends in the evening, had to become the habitué of a salon. The idea of spending an intimate evening at home simply didn't occur to Parisian couples. Besides, hostesses didn't like to receive husband and wife together; that, they said, put a damper on the conversation. To escape the insipidity of conjugal exchanges, each partner had to go off to a different salon where there would be no reminders of duty's chains."

Given the mores of the time, Girardin's romantic adventures were no doubt seen both by him and by Delphine as attempts to prove himself a *"galant homme"* and to escape the public ridicule associated with being a faithful husband. The natural corollary, one might suppose, would be for Delphine to seek consolation elsewhere. She was, after all, in the prime of life, a charming and beautiful woman. Yet there is little evidence that she was ever tempted to stray from strict fidelity. Once, a handsome young boulevardier was so smitten that he begged her to run off abroad with him and dramatically threatened suicide if she refused. She did refuse; he shot himself. Aside from that episode, there is only the dubious anecdote picked up and recorded by those egregious gossip-mongers Edmond and Jules de Goncourt. "One of Girardin's friends says to him: 'Present me to your wife.' —'Gladly.' He leads the friend to his wife's room, opens the door, quickly closes it, saying: 'Impossible! She's in bed with Monsieur M., who is horribly jealous.'" But the Goncourts could never resist a juicy story, either true or apocryphal.

Delphine served her husband, and her own renown, not only through her salon, but also through her weekly column in Girardin's *La Presse*. Using the pseudonym Vicomte de Launay, she contributed a series of free-wheeling commentaries on life in Parisian high society, with titillating glimpses into the secrets of the élite. Nothing quite like these "Parisian Letters" had been tried before; they had something in common with the gossip columns of our own day, though they ventured more freely into generalizations on manners and mores. The "Letters" won a devoted readership at once, and further boosted the circulation figures of *La Presse*. The real identity of the Vicomte de Launay was soon guessed, adding still more to her worldly reputation. Some modern critics exalt the "Letters" as her finest work, and praise them as an unrivaled portrait of life in the social stratosphere during the July monarchy. After Delphine's untimely death, the "Letters" were reprinted as part of her *Collected Works*: they take up two of the six stout volumes.

Delphine herself once suggested, with a touch of irony, that what she called her "collection of chit-chat" might some day become a source for historians. "We columnists," she wrote, "are to the historian what the dabbling student is to the painter, the hod-carrier to the mason, the pot-boy to the chef. Our metier ought to have a name; we don't know the right word, but it ought to exist; perhaps it is journalist." In a teasing mood, she put the historians in their place: "The history of the past is easy enough to write; with only a bit of imagination one can manage; but the history of the present is far more difficult. To observe and to understand at the same time isn't simple."

Whether or not the "Parisian Letters" are the historian's best source for the city's high life in her day, they do provide us with insights into Delphine's character and beliefs. Her instincts, like those of her husband, were intensely libertarian and ferociously anti-equalitarian. "Ah! what bliss to be free, free in the most beautiful sense of the word, liberty of thought; to bear the chains of no party, to be independent of those in power yet free of any alliance with their enemies; to be spared the need to defend stupidity on the one hand and bad faith on the other." But equality she denounced as a delusive snare; nature distributed her gifts unequally, whereupon society tried to cancel out these true differences by setting up such artificial measures as those of wealth, education, and birthright. The times, she complained, were dominated by two rival but interlinked passions, "the monomania of equality and the thirst for luxury. What do our young and ferocious republicans do as soon as they get a bit of money? They furnish an apartment in Louis XV style. And they suppress royalty and aristocracy, abolish the family and property, and call for thousands of heads to fall."

In a lighter and more ironic vein, she addressed the question of the French character. Critics, she said, were quite wrong in calling the French a frivolous people. "We, frivolous? No people anywhere is so serious, so routine-minded, so addicted to habits. A frivolous character is one that is changeable; but with us nothing changes; we sometimes try a different king, but nothing else; our pleasures don't vary, our tastes are eternal, our fashions are deplorably stable."

But a different tone marked her comments on the position of women in France; her irony was tinged with bitterness. True, she ruled out anything more than a backstage role for women in politics, praising the conduct of her rival hostess Madame de Lieven, who "has chosen the only political role proper for a woman—she doesn't act, she inspires those who act; in her salon she reigns but does not govern." But when some man teasingly suggested that a token woman or two be admitted to the Académie Française, her irritation overflowed. "Why grant a privilege to women who have been denied all rights?" she demanded. What Frenchmen want in their women is "resignation." They preach adoration of women but practice malevolence when they establish the rules. Why? Because they are envious of Frenchwomen who, they know, are more intelligent than they. In fact, ever since the Frankish conquest men and women have been mortal enemies, each seeking personal domination. "A Frenchman loves only those women for whom he has a certain contempt. They alone will be pardoned for having more wit than he possesses." Superior intelligence "explains the immense influence of women in this country, where they enjoy so little authority, where they amount to nothing; there is not a man in Paris or in the provinces whose actions don't respond to the will of a woman. Women have attained such influence by the use of duplicity and innocent hypocrisy; they have docilely accepted the modest role imposed on them in order to conceal their ambition for an important role; they have veiled their superiority and have thus reassured their tyrants." Why, then, should women aspire to such honors as the Académie? "Keep the learned chairs for yourselves, gentlemen; for women who are modestly resigned to their condition, a footstool is enough." Despite her playful tone, Delphine may be suspected of betraying here some personal discontents. "Resignation" is an apt term for her relationship with Girardin; it enabled her to influence her husband's political and journalistic activities more effectively than he himself realized.

The revolution of 1848 disrupted life in the Girardin household. Girardin hoped to save the monarchy through setting up a regency, but saw that hope quickly swept away by the triumph of the Second Republic. Although both Girardins had always been hostile to the idea of a republic, they were briefly converted to the new regime; Girardin's editorial support in *La Presse* brought many members of the well-to-do bourgeoisie into the republican fold. But Girardin expected more from the republican leaders than they were ready to give. He deluged the provisional government with reform proposals, and expected to receive a ministerial post from which to impose his ideas. No offer came; frustrated, he soon retreated from his republican aberration. Delphine chimed in too; in her final column in 1848, she commented bitterly: "How beautiful the republic would be, if only there were no republicans." Girardin transferred his hopes to

Louis-Napoleon Bonaparte, candidate for the presidency of the republic; but soon after Bonaparte won the election Girardin found the new president wanting. When Louis-Napoleon in 1851 carried out his coup d'état, Girardin was outraged, and was exiled for a time to Brussels. When he was allowed to return, *La Presse* was so hamstrung by new press laws that his journalistic voice was stilled.

Delphine throughout these years had loyally supported her husband's political choices, and had joined him in brief exile. After their return she continued to play hostess to her literary friends (except for those like Victor Hugo, exiled in Jersey), but her soirées were smaller and more informal now. At the same time, she enjoyed a new season of literary success; three of her plays were produced and acclaimed at the Théâtre-Français, two others at a leading boulevard theater. She was caught up also in the current craze for "table-turning" among the social élite, and won some notoriety as a medium who could commune with the spirit world. But her friends were aware that a mysterious illness was sapping her energies; since the late 1840s she had been suffering from what came to be diagnosed as stomach cancer. She bore her affliction with fortitude, continuing to write and to circulate in society; if she knew that Girardin had embarked on a new liaison with the actress Rachel, she gave no sign. The disease conquered her at last in 1855, at the age of fifty-one. She was mourned by a wide circle of friends and, quite certainly, by her philandering husband as well. Girardin's tribute to Delphine was the publication of her complete works in six handsome volumes. He married again (unsuccessfully) and lived on until 1881— long enough to see the fall of Emperor Napoleon III and to regain a seat in the Third Republic's Parliament. In his latter years, Girardin recovered much but not all of the influence he had enjoyed during the July monarchy. Perhaps he came to realize that his greatest successes had owed much to Delphine's presence. With her tact and charm, she could compensate for his cold aloofness and his awkwardness in social relations.

Girardin chose to be buried in Montmartre cemetery alongside

Delphine, under a shared gravestone that bore the legend, "Death separated them, death has reunited them." On the broader stage of Parisian life, Delphine's passing ended a brilliant chapter in the history of that celebrated Parisian institution, the literary salon. Other hostesses were to succeed her; none would outshine her.

2

Eugène Sue
Master of the Serial Thriller

E ighteen hundred four was a good year, and January a boun-
tiful month. One day after Delphine Gay's birth in Aix-la-Chapelle,
a male child was born in Paris, to be known as Eugène Sue. The lives
of Delphine and Eugène began one day apart, and ended less than
two years apart; between those marker-dates they followed parallel
lines that intersected at times. Both of them were to attain celebrity
status in the Parisian world of their day; both were to win a wide
public as popular writers. Sue's audience, however, was both broader
and vastly larger. At the height of his career in the 1840s, he was
almost certainly the most widely read author in France, and his works
were translated—and pirated—throughout Europe. Almost everyone read Sue, or at least knew his name.

Sue was no outsider, forced to scratch his own way up the ladder
to success. He was a silver-spoon child, whose future fortunes
seemed assured from the moment of birth. He came of a line of
distinguished surgeons which, since the days of Louis XIV, had
provided Paris with a dozen eminent doctors. Eugène's father, the
most recent of these medical luminaries, enjoyed a lucrative practice

13

and useful governmental connections. One of Eugène's godparents was Josephine, first wife of Napoleon Bonaparte. Everyone took for granted that the newborn son would prolong the Sue medical dynasty well through the nineteenth century.

Alas for tradition, and for the family's hopes! From the start, Eugène showed himself a fractious child. Enrolled in the best Parisian *lycée,* he and a few rebellious classmates found the classroom boring, and the city streets far more alluring. The elder Sue, exasperated by the boy's waywardness, scolded and threatened, but to no effect; Eugène persisted in his erring ways. At last Sue *père* withdrew him from the *lycée* and condemned him to learn doctoring the hard way, as a kind of apprentice in the hospital directed by Dr. Sue himself. Some rudiments of medical science rubbed off, but Eugène found ways to evade paternal supervision and to join his band of young friends in their nocturnal adventures. One night they raided Dr. Sue's cellar and were discovered in the garden swilling his most prized vintages. Enough was enough; Dr. Sue got Eugène assigned as a surgeon's aide in the army. Adventure followed; Eugène took part in the invasion of Spain (1823) where the French army, on behalf of the European powers, was engaged in chastising the subversive Spanish liberals. The army returned victorious, without having fought a battle. Eugène gloried in the role of hero, and plunged full time into the high life of Paris. With his band of friends, he haunted the fashionable cafés and theaters, entertained lavishly, and found complaisant young ladies to share his pleasures. In Balzacian fashion, he paid for these bohemian pursuits by resorting to pawnbrokers and usurers, and by signing the equivalent of IOU's. But as the bills came due and landed on his father's desk, the furious Dr. Sue resorted again to desperate measures. This time he sent Eugène off to the navy, on the theory that this would keep him far away from Paris for a long time. As an assistant surgeon on a warship, he cruised the seas of the world for almost six years, from 1824 to 1829. He visited exotic shores from the South Seas to the West Indies, and even experienced battle. He was present at

Navarino in 1827, when the European fleets annihilated those of Turkey and Egypt. From these years of naval service, he was to draw the inspiration for his early novels.

Twice during those years at sea, Eugène was granted lengthy leaves of absence to deal with "urgent family matters." The urgency, in fact, was merely his nostalgia for the bohemian life of Paris with his old cronies and a set of new socialite acquaintances. For a time he thought that painting would be his true vocation; for a couple of years he haunted the studio of a successful artist friend. He dabbled in writing too, especially for the theater, and made contacts in the literary world. He became a favored guest at Sophie Gay's salon; there was even talk of a possible romance with Delphine— or, since his tastes were catholic, with Delphine's sister, or perhaps her best friend. He met Balzac, and formed a friendship that remained close for some years. He encountered Delphine's husband Emile de Girardin, and was invited to contribute a piece to Girardin's new weekly *La Mode*. Handsome and self-assured, a typical dandy in dress and manner, he was rated as a successful young man about town. All he lacked was a bottomless purse to cover his expenses; and that deficiency was soon corrected. In 1830 his maternal grandfather died, leaving him 80,000 francs; and better still, his father soon passed to his reward, providing him with an inheritance of 700,000 francs. A fortune of that size placed Sue in the top 0.02 percent of the French population. He promptly resigned his naval commission, abandoned his marginal interest in medicine, and settled happily into his destiny as a rich young playboy. The necessary appurtenances of that life were soon acquired: a splendid apartment in the heart of Paris, a tilbury with a pair of dashing horses, and a mistress with a worldly reputation. The high-level courtesan whose *nom de guerre* was Olympe Pelissier filled the bill perfectly, though Eugène had to share her with other admirers.

The playboy life, however, took up only part of Sue's energies. In the salon-and-café circle in which he moved, it was *bon ton* to show a bit of literary talent. From dabbling in light comedies for the

boulevard theaters, Sue moved to somewhat more serious efforts—
a series of adventure novels that drew on his experience at sea. His
tales were full of action, and his heroes colorful rascals: pirates,
smugglers, slave-traders, privateers. The exotic appeal of these novels won him a considerable readership; some critics hailed him as
"France's James Fenimore Cooper." He was taken up now by an
even more elegant sector of Parisian society—certain duchesses of
the Faubourg Saint-Germain, who prided themselves on their exclusive literary salons. Sue's indifference to political and social issues
(he professed a kind of amoral skepticism that verged on the cynical)
made it easy for him to adopt the values and biases of his new
aristocratic patronesses; he took on the legitimist line of the ultra-
conservatives and denounced the self-seeking revolutionists of 1789.
It is not surprising that when the exclusive new Jockey Club was
founded in 1835, Sue was one of the first applicants admitted. Sue
also broadened his friendships in the cultural world of Paris to
include such notables as George Sand, Marie d'Agoult, the critic
Sainte-Beuve, and the composers Liszt, Chopin, and Berlioz.

Despite these brilliant social and literary successes, Sue in the
later 1830s was heading into a somewhat premature midlife crisis.
It was foreshadowed by his first literary failure. He conceived the
idea of a ten-volume history of the French navy, as a bid for serious
scholarly recognition. Although colorful and anecdotal, it was a
patchwork product put together mainly by hired assistants, and it
earned a cool reception. Sue's confidence was shaken, and his energies flagged for a time. Worse still, his spendthrift habits finally
caught up with him; his inheritance had been used up and his debts
were enormous; he even feared debtors' prison. The change in his
fortunes led his fair-weather friends to fall away; he was dropped
from the Jockey Club for nonpayment of dues. There was gossip
that he had run out of ideas, and that Sue himself knew that his
literary career was finished. He even considered suicide, but admitted that he lacked the courage for that desperate act. He cut
back his life-style drastically, and cast about for some way out.

The solution arrived just in time; it was to open the path for Sue's greatest successes. The new vehicle for fame and fortune was to be the feuilleton—the serial novel which for some time had been a modest feature of the French periodical press. It was Emile de Girardin, along with one of his rival press entrepreneurs, whose genius detected the feuilleton's possibilities. His idea was to sign up the most celebrated authors of the time, offering them generous contracts and a mass audience. So successful was the scheme that other publishers joined in; during the 1840s the feuilleton became the rage. Newspaper offices were besieged by readers eager for copies hot off the press; reading rooms (*cabinets de lecture*) enjoyed a bonanza, charging a fee for a quarter-hour's access to the latest installment.

The feuilleton perfectly suited Sue's talents; his pen was facile and his imagination fertile. The challenge of producing weekly chapters jolted him out of the doldrums and restored his finances. He worked with an energy that astonished his friends; his serialized novels were promptly issued as multivolume books, and then converted into plays that drew crowds to the boulevard theaters. Yet he found time to resume an active social life; his old friend Delphine Gay de Girardin, in one of her "Parisian Letters," marveled at his enormous capacity for both work and pleasure.

Sue's first feuilleton, called *Arthur*, published in Girardin's *La Presse*, revealed a strain of self-analysis. His hero was a handsome young playboy, lionized in high society, but hiding his true nature beneath a mask of cynicism. That mask was torn away when Arthur found love; his generous and high-minded impulses prevailed, and he abandoned the life of dandy for that of philanthropist. If Sue saw himself in Arthur, this may explain the turn that his life now took. The success of *Arthur* led other publishers to bid for his services; his next novel, *The Mysteries of Paris,* was bought by the conservative daily *Le Constitutionnel*, and increased that journal's circulation overnight from 3,600 to 20,000. It represented a dramatic change of focus, from his early works of exotic maritime adventure and his subsequent tales of high society to the proletarian world of eastern Paris. One night in 1841 Sue met at the theater the ebullient Felix Pyat, a second-rate playwright and novelist of republican-socialist beliefs. Pyat, whom one eminent historian has labeled "that monumental ass," persuaded Sue to join him the next evening at the home of a workingman of his acquaintance. The experience was a revelation: the simplicity and warmth of his host's family circle, the passion and brilliance with which this self-educated worker held forth on the proletarian condition and on socialist formulas for a better society, left Sue transfixed. "I am a socialist!" he cried at the end of the evening. His conversion, in fact, was neither so immediate nor so total as this episode might suggest; he knew next to nothing of the mysterious and exotic world of the Parisian workers, or of the socialist ideas emerging in that era. Yet he was now awakened to a hitherto unsuspected universe that lay only a few streets away from the bourgeois and aristocratic quarters where his life until now had been spent. That exotic universe was to provide the setting for the novels that would rank as his greatest successes.

The Mysteries of Paris appeared serially in *Le Constitutionnel* in 1842–43, and caused an immediate and lasting sensation. Adapted for the theater, it was the season's smash hit. "Parisians," wrote Delphine Gay, "talk of nothing else; Sue is the toast of Paris." This enormous, sprawling, melodramatic epic, set in the noisome slums that adjoined Notre Dame Cathedral, presented a cast of characters from the lower depths of the urban jungle. Haunting the streets and grog-shops of the quarter was a population of drifters, petty thieves, confidence men, and vicious criminals, all desperately seeking to survive. Among them, in shining contrast, stood the beautiful and pure-hearted maiden called Fleur-de-Marie, valiantly resisting the corrupting pressures that had driven her to a life of prostitution. And to her rescue came a superhuman hero, Rodolphe of Gerolstein, a German prince in workingman's disguise. Rodolphe's shadowy connection with the police was less important than his inner source of authority—his awesome physical strength and his charismatic personality. Righteousness and justice were arrayed against the forces of evil, the latter personified in the grasping, lustful notary Jacques Ferrand. For a time, the scene of action shifted to a farm outside Paris, where a Fourierist community lived in harmonious association, contrasting sharply with the Parisian jungle. After innumerable hair-raising adventures and narrow escapes, Fleur-de-Marie was saved by Rodolphe from the clutches of her exploiters, restored to a life of virtuous purity, and discovered to be Rodolphe's long-lost daughter.

Sue made some attempt to acquaint himself with the scene of the "mysteries." In workman's clothing, he roamed the urban slums at night, accompanied by his instructors in boxing and *savate* (a kind of karate), who had been giving him preparatory lessons in the manly arts. But Sue's search was for atmosphere and local color rather than for realistic detail. His novel calls to mind some modern comic strips, or the early film serials whose episodes always ended with the heroine in fearful peril. His characters were two-dimensional, embodiments of the extremes in evil and virtue. Yet such flaws could not deter the millions of avid French readers, nor the crowds of European and American devotees, who became hypnotically attached to Sue's fast-paced thriller. For bourgeois Parisians, here was a new and exotic world located not on a distant continent but only a few streets away; Sue offered them an armchair tour of an unknown Paris. For working-class readers, who often listened while one of their literate fellows read aloud, their miseries were exposed in a spirit of sympathy and hope. As the novel moved toward its denouement, Sue's new stance as social reformer became more explicit; at times he interrupted the narrative to lecture his readers on the need for a new society of harmony and justice. For many of Sue's earlier admirers, this was dangerously subversive talk; they saw him as a renegade to his class. But the socialist sects applauded this celebrated convert; all factions claimed him as their own. On the left, only Karl Marx angrily rejected and ridiculed what he saw as Sue's flabby humanitarianism. Sue was flattered by the adulation of the socialists, and even contributed brief items to their newspapers; but he refused a formal commitment to any sect, and remained eclectic in his beliefs.

The enormous success of *The Mysteries* turned Sue into a major celebrity, a European phenomenon. Correspondents both French and foreign deluged him with praise, advice, appeals for help; pirated translations of *The Mysteries* appeared in most European countries. His fame cost him the friendship of his old comrade Balzac, jealous of his rival's notoriety. On the other hand, it won him an extended contract from the publisher of *Le Correspondant*, which had been rescued from bankruptcy by Sue's novel. Sue accepted a fourteen-year contract to contribute an annual feuilleton at 100,000 francs each—an unprecedented bonanza for a novelist of that day. He embarked at once on his next project, which was to become his second great popular success.

The Wandering Jew, published in 1844–45, resembled *The Mysteries* in many respects. Much of the action again occurred in the slums of eastern Paris; the characters continued to personify either good or evil, with little or no shading; and in the end, righteousness again triumphed, though some of the heroes were sacrificed on the way. But there were differences too. For one thing, a touch of the fantastic was introduced in the form of two biblical characters, the Wandering Jew and Herodiad, both of whom were condemned to roam the world forever, and were thus available to rescue the virtuous from the jaws of disaster. Another difference was the novel's more impassioned advocacy of a transformed society, both in the form of more frequent interludes of outright preaching, and in the introduction of a saintly factory owner, a Saint-Simonian-cum-Fourierist captain of industry who transformed his enterprise along utopian lines. Still a third novelty was the effective use of a real episode still fresh in the memory of Parisians—the appalling cholera epidemic that devastated the proletarian quarters in the early 1830s. Finally—and most striking—was Sue's hostile treatment of the Church, and especially his choice of the Jesuits as arch-villains. His portrayal of the Jesuits was unsparing: they were described as malignant conspirators slavishly served by secret agents "in short robes" throughout Europe, and dedicated to achieving absolute world power. The mastermind of this conspiracy, the Jesuit Rodin, surely belongs among the most fearsome and despicable villains of all literature. Sue's plunge into Jesuitophobia reflected a powerful current of anticlerical paranoia in the France of his time; the historians Michelet and Quinet, in their lectures at the Collège de France, were engaged in a similar anti-Jesuit crusade at the same time. No doubt *The Wandering Jew* added intensity to the bloodless civil war that was to divide Frenchmen for the next half-century. Sue did, however, provide a counterweight in the form of the priest Gabriel, a truly angelic figure who embodied Sue's idea of true Christianity, free of dogma and greed.

The Wandering Jew reinforced Sue's reputation as the master of the serialized thriller. His following remained enormous, and the pirated translations continued to spread his fame. But his more belligerent commitment to a vague socialism and to "priest-eating" alienated most of his former friends and readers of conservative bent. He had emerged now as the recognized symbol and standard-bearer of the left. But he still had no interest in entering the political arena directly. His aloofness was to continue until it was shaken by the revolution that brought down the monarchy in February 1848.

Sue's ablest biographer, Jean-Louis Bory, insists that Sue was one of the inspirers of that revolution; indeed, Bory labels it "the revolution of the feuilleton." Sue and a few other popular novelists, he contends, awakened the masses to the need for political and social change, and brought them into the streets to demand a program of sweeping reforms. The case is plausible, though probably exaggerated. The feuilletonists were not the only exponents of change who were undermining the bourgeois monarchy. But Sue undoubtedly won new converts to the cause of social democracy; his novels offered a romantic vision of a better world in which exploitation would give way to brotherhood.

The February revolution found Sue at his farm in the Loire Valley, where he had been spending much of his time in recent years. That rural retreat enabled him to devote his total energies to his massive writing commitments: *The Wandering Jew* had been followed by *Martin the Foundling*, then by the first in a sequence of seven novels devoted to the seven deadly sins. Sue's immense popularity on the left seemed to dictate some kind of leadership role for him in the new republic, but he remained reluctant. In place of activism, he preferred to devote some of his energy and resources to distributing charity for the poor in his rural area, and to writing and circulating a propaganda brochure at his own expense, designed to win the peasantry to the social republic. His pamphlet proposed a reform program that still resonates in our time: day-care centers for the children of workers, shelters for the aged indigent, extensive public works, free and universal education, a progressive tax system, a guarantee of jobs for all, and the ideal of association as the solution to class conflict. In April, when elections were held for a Constituent Assembly, Sue was persuaded by his admirers to let his name be put up in his rural district. But his peasant neighbors were suspicious of this urban interloper who talked like a socialist but lived like an aristocrat. He was soundly beaten, and accepted defeat with relief.

Sue was dismayed, however, by the rising dissension that now threatened to tear the new republic apart. The Constituent Assembly, dominated by conservatives, set out at once to repeal the regime's initial reforms; and the result was the June Days, a bloody three-day civil war in the streets of Paris. The Assembly used the army to crush the rebellion: much of the working-class and democratic-socialist leadership was wiped out at the barricades. Those leftists who escaped prison or exile pinned their remaining hopes on the election of a president, scheduled for December. Sue plunged into the campaign with another brochure justifying the program of the so-called "democ-soc" candidates, whom conservatives preferred to label "reds." He repeated his list of social reforms needed to transform

France, but adopted a clearer stance in defense of property, extolling the Fourierist idea of association while rejecting Etienne Cabet's scheme of communal ownership. Again, failure: by a landslide the voters swept Louis-Napoleon Bonaparte into the presidency.

Nevertheless, Sue's venture into active politics was still ahead. The "democ-socs," though badly weakened, continued to organize and agitate both in the press and in the republic's new parliament. A vacancy in Parliament in 1850 brought a by-election in Paris, and the democ-soc leaders there turned to Sue as their candidate. Again he hesitated, then consented; and after a campaign marked by some violence and much vilification, he won a narrow victory. He was beaten in the bourgeois and aristocratic quarters, but triumphed thanks to the working-class and lower middle-class districts. His election produced a brief panic on the stock market, and contributed to Parliament's subsequent decision to restrict universal male suffrage by denying the vote to much of the proletariat. For the propertied classes, Sue had become a menacing symbol of social upheaval.

Sue was forty-six when he entered public life for the first and only time. He had always doubted his fitness for such a role, and his conduct in Parliament soon confirmed those doubts. Sue's pen was fluent and tireless, but before an audience he was tongue-tied, and he lacked any talent for cutting deals backstage. Not once in a year and a half did he rise to speak in a parliamentary debate. His enemies indulged in ironic jokes about his silence, and alleged that he spent his time during sessions reading proofs of his novels. His democ-soc sponsors were disappointed, but they were busily engaged in planning and organizing for the next parliamentary elections in 1852. The prospect of "red" gains in those elections frightened the bourgeoisie and played into the hands of President Bonaparte, whose single term was due to end shortly. On the night of December 2, 1851 the president carried out a coup d'état that ended the Second Republic in all but name. The Assembly was dissolved and the opposition leaders arrested; many were soon ordered into exile.

Sue, not surprisingly, was one of those arrested and jailed for a short time, yet in the end he was not formally exiled. At one point his name appeared on a list of radicals to be shipped to the French penal colony in Guiana, but that order was mysteriously cancelled. It is likely that one of Sue's old acquaintances in Bonaparte's entourage intervened on his behalf. Although Sue was at liberty to remain in France, he insisted on sharing the fate of his fellow democ-socs; he departed for the neighboring kingdom of Savoy, and settled down quietly to live out his declining years in the sleepy town of Annecy.

Once gone from Paris, Sue was never allowed to return. The Savoyard authorities required him to avoid all political activity; they wanted no trouble with France. Sue resumed his lifetime habit of non-stop writing, eight to ten hours a day, though the Paris newspapers soon found it prudent to reject his feuilletons, and the publisher of *Le Correspondent* bought off Sue's long-term contract. The heyday of the feuilleton, in any case, was over, and Sue's popular appeal was in decline. He embarked on a massive novel called *The Mysteries of the People* which, he thought, would be his masterpiece and his chief contribution to building a new world. The story purported to carry the history of a proletarian family from the origins of humanity to a euphoric state of universal brotherhood and harmony, anticipated for the near future. This final novel was issued piecemeal on a subscription basis. Many of his longtime readers subscribed, but most were disappointed. The theme was stale, the old fire gone.

Sue in exile was a lonely man, increasingly forgotten except by the conservatives who saw him as a satanic threat. Occasionally other political exiles dropped by to visit. He conducted a sporadic correspondence with such old friends as Delphine Gay de Girardin until her death in 1855; and he was consoled by a platonic, almost paternal relationship with a glamorous young widow of twenty, Marie de Solms, a granddaughter of Lucien Bonaparte who had fallen out with her distant cousin Napoleon III and had settled in nearby Aix-les-Bains. Although barely past fifty, he was beset by premature aging; his once robust health deteriorated rapidly, perhaps from years of overwork, perhaps from youthful excesses. In 1857 a massive stroke cut him down, but controversy followed him to the grave and beyond. Some anticlericals suspected that the Jesuits had done him in by slow poisoning; some conservatives hinted at syphilis contracted in youth. A group of political exiles hoped to turn his funeral into a public demonstration against Napoleon III, but the Savoyard prime minister, Count Cavour, ordered the police to keep strict order. Sue's funeral procession to the cemetery in Annecy was followed by a few personal friends and more than a thousand loyal admirers. There was talk of commissioning a statue to be placed in Annecy, but furious protests from Catholic spokesmen scotched that plan. Another half-century would pass before Sue could receive his Annecy monument—a Rodin-like statue of the Wandering Jew, financed by public subscription and installed in 1907 over violent conservative protests. The city of Paris had already granted him its form of immortality: in 1885 a new street on the northern slope of Montmartre (appropriately, a working-class quarter) was baptized rue Eugène-Sue.

Posterity has not dealt very generously with Eugène Sue. As the historian Dominique De Santi has remarked, time has turned Sue into little more than a "sociological curiosity." It is easy to understand why historians and critics of literature have denied him a place in the pantheon of his great contemporaries—Balzac, Hugo, Flaubert, Dumas, George Sand. His work was seriously flawed by excessive sentimentalism, an unbridled imagination, and a frequent indifference to form and style. His characters lacked depth, and his plots too often required a suspension of belief. Yet for a decade Sue was the most widely read of French writers, and his impact on the political and social sentiments of his countrymen probably exceeded that of any other writer of fiction in his time. Indeed, he has kept a reduced but faithful audience right down to our own day, though mainly among juveniles thirsting for adventure. No doubt part of his work's appeal was that of all escape literature: it gave readers a way to evade the boredom of daily existence. But he also tapped a vein of sensibility to problems of the day, and awakened many Frenchmen to the injustices lurking behind the comfortable middle-class facade. An unfriendly historian, Pierre Chaunu, has described Sue as the truest representative of the so-called men of 1848 "because of his very mediocrity." His caustic remark may contain some truth, but it brushes aside Sue's commitment to exposing and challenging social injustice. Sue, despite his serious failings, meant well, tried to understand and to change his world. Not all of his contemporaries, and not all of those moderns who disparage him, can say as much.

3

Allan Kardec
Apostle of Spiritism

Amidcentury visitor to Paris might have been bemused to find so many Parisians caught up in the latest craze—the practice of what its adepts called spiritism. A new professional cadre of mediums emerged into the limelight; séances came to be a standard form of entertainment in the drawing rooms of both high and bourgeois society. Many participants were attracted by nothing more than curiosity and the desire to be *à la page*; but a considerable number of Parisians, like Delphine Gay, and the exiled Victor Hugo, became true believers and active practitioners. There is no sure explanation for the speed and breadth of spiritism's growth. For some adherents, it probably offered an escape from the arid certainties of materialism as embodied in the rise of positivist doctrine. Romanticism had become passé, but had left behind a thirst for something that would satisfy men's emotions and sense of awe when confronted by the unknown. But the success of spiritism was also built on a widespread interest in the occult, dating at least from the whirlwind Parisian career of the Austrian physician Dr. Franz Mesmer.

Mesmer opened his clinic in 1778 and achieved a sensational

success. "Mesmerism" earned the doctor a small fortune before his critics succeeded in closing down his practice and driving him into Swiss retirement. He claimed to have discovered the existence of a fluid that surrounded and penetrated all bodies, and whose flow through the human body was essential for health. Sickness was caused by an obstacle to the flow of the vital fluid; it could be corrected by "mesmerizing" or massaging the patient to bring on epileptic-like fits or hypnotic trances. The body was seen as analogous to a magnet; and Mesmer claimed to possess a power which he called "animal magnetism" by which he could effect cures. He also invented a device to store the life-giving fluid: tubs were filled with iron filings and bottles of mesmerized water arranged like the spokes of a wheel; patients sat around the tub in a chain, communicating the fluid to one another. Occasionally, mesmerized subjects reported communication with spirits who sent messages by way of the vital fluid. Mesmerism, generally rechristened animal magnetism, survived the downfall of its creator; it experienced a considerable revival in Paris during the 1840s, when a society of believers was organized and a monthly journal was founded. The popularity of magnetism prepared the way for spiritism.

Reports of spiritist manifestations arrived in France from the New World in the early 1850s. A family named Fox in upper New York State had been annoyed by spirit rappings in their home, and the two teenage Fox daughters had developed mediumistic talents that allowed them to communicate with the disturbing spirits. With the help of neighbors, they worked out devices and codes that made the communication process more efficient—notably by the use of small round tables that turned, leaped about, and tapped out messages. The Fox sisters took their show on the road, traveling widely and demonstrating their occult abilities. Hundreds of imitators soon followed their example; spirit-rappings and table-turning spread across the country. By 1853 spiritism arrived in France, and found a ready clientele. Here, too, mediums proliferated, and developed more rapid techniques for conversing with the spirit world. In place of the tiresome tapping codes (one tap for A, twenty-six for Z), devices were invented to permit direct spirit-writing. Delphine Gay de Girardin created another model (later called the Girardin Table) which resembled the device that bore the name Ouija Board.

Despite its immediate popularity, spiritism might have remained a mere nine-day wonder had it not been for the organizational and public relations talents of a French schoolmaster named Hippolyte Rivail. Born in Lyon in 1804, Rivail came of solid bourgeois stock; his father was a minor legal official. At age ten the boy was packed off to Switzerland to be educated in the famous experimental school founded by the reformer Pestalozzi. He spent several years under the tutelage of this disciple of Rousseau, whose goal was to inspire a thirst for learning through the use of radically new methods. Pestalozzi replaced the classics by a modern scientific curriculum, emphasizing the direct observation of nature and the systematizing of knowledge. The master's personal example, as a high-minded reformer and moralist, no doubt left its mark on such students as Rivail. The young man responded with enthusiasm to this challenging opportunity; he learned three modern languages in addition to French, and developed an enduring taste for analyzing and classifying. The Pestalozzi method, which assigned older students to tutor younger ones, also gave him his first teaching experience, and pointed him toward a schoolmaster's career. The only distasteful aspect of his Swiss school days was the mild hazing he as a Catholic received from his Protestant fellow students. His discomfort left him with a determination to develop a universal religion that would transcend such sectarian differences. It was his moral duty, he believed, to crusade for a world of enlightenment, brotherhood, and peace.

Young Rivail set out early to put his ideas into action. In 1825 he published a tract on the reform of public education which embodied pedagogical ideas far ahead of their time and which won a prize from a provincial academy. It went unnoticed, however, by the educational establishment. One passage in this essay was startling when read in the light of his later career. The study of the sciences, he wrote, must be the heart of the process; it "will make men laugh at the superstitious credulity of their ignorant fellows. They will no longer believe in ghosts and phantoms. They will no longer take will-o'-the-wisps for spirits." That faith in science Rivail never abandoned; spiritism, he always insisted after his conversion to that creed, was itself a science based on the direct observation of natural phenomena.

Meanwhile, thanks to a loan from a prosperous uncle, Rivail had established a Pestalozzian school in Paris, and directed it for almost a decade. At age twenty-eight he married a teacher nine years his senior, with prospects of a handsome inheritance. Life seemed promising for this dedicated couple of hard-working pedagogues. But destiny suddenly turned hostile. The uncle, ruined by gambling, demanded repayment of the loan, which forced liquidation of the school. Then Madame Rivail's inheritance was wiped out by the bankruptcy of their investment counselor. Penniless, they faced up courageously to disaster. Rivail, whose drive and energy were always phenomenal, settled in daily at his desk at 4:30 in the morning. He taught himself accountancy, and for the next twenty years kept the books of several small businesses. In his free time, he embarked on a career of textbook writing, publishing school manuals on arithmetic, grammar, and other subjects. His talent for systematizing lent itself to success in that enterprise; some of his textbooks went through numerous editions and continued to sell until the end of the century. These activities earned him a modest scholarly reputation, enough to admit him to several marginal learned societies and to enable him to teach occasional courses in a *lycée*. Both Rivail and his wife continued to be moved by a kind of missionary urge to teach; they found time to offer free courses in various sciences in their apartment at 8 rue des Martyrs.

At the age of fifty, Rivail could console himself with the thought that he had attained a kind of petit bourgeois success. He and his wife lived comfortably but parsimoniously; they had no children or close relatives and few intimate friends. The political and cultural life of Paris they ignored; they showed no interest in the upheavals that disrupted French life as the country moved from monarchy to republic to empire. Rivail had apparently given up his youthful dreams of reforming the educational system or creating a new universal religion. For more than twenty years he had been reduced to the life of a scholarly drudge, devoting his energies to accountancy and textbook writing—a dual career guaranteed to dry up the springs of imagination and initiative. To anticipate a dramatic change of life for such a man would seem to verge on fantasy. Yet this man, Hippolyte Rivail, was to be transmuted during his last fifteen years into a kind of messiah who at his death claimed a million followers both within and beyond the borders of France.

It was in May 1855 that Rivail was first enticed into attending a spiritist séance. For a year he had evaded the urgings of a couple of acquaintances that he observe for himself the phenomenon that was exciting so many Parisians. Although he had been intrigued by magnetism and somnambulism (hypnotism) for thirty-five years, as he later recalled, the idea of tables that revolved and spoke left him skeptical. When he visited a séance at last, he was impressed by the solid and serious mien of the participants; he had rather expected to find cranks and charlatans. His skepticism persisted, however, until one evening the medium summoned forth a spirit who declared that he had known Rivail in a previous existence. Two thousand years earlier, in the time of the Gauls, this spirit claimed to have known him as a Breton Druid named Allan Kardec. Rivail was sufficiently impressed to continue attending séances, and to accept the task of putting some order into the voluminous records compiled by various mediums during the previous couple of years. As he proceeded with this task, his analytical bent led him to confront the spirits via the mediums with a host of questions about the nature of the spirit world and the relationship between the spirits and living persons. His last doubts were overcome when a spirit designated him by name as destined to undertake a grave mission: to prepare a new universal religion for the coming day of apocalypse when the world would be destroyed and instantly replaced by a brand new world. Buoyed by this endorsement, Rivail redoubled his efforts; the spirits of the greatest of saints and scholars—Saint Augustine, Saint Louis, Socrates, Plato, Fénelon, Franklin "etc., etc."—were quizzed in detail on every major or minor point that occurred to him.

Out of this exhaustive effort came a volume of almost 900 pages called the *Book of Spirits*, edited not by Hippolyte Rivail but by Allan Kardec. The real authors, he explained in a long introduction, were the eminent spirits who had generously responded to his questions; the manuscript had then been reviewed and corrected by those same spirits. But the form of the final product bore the unmistakable earmarks of its editor. Constructed in the form of a catechism—1018 questions with brief or lengthy answers—the volume had obviously been put together by an experienced author of textbooks, and by someone with a passion for systematizing and classifying. In an early chapter, for example, the inhabitants of the spirit world were described by grouping them into three broad categories—imperfect, good, and pure spirits, in ascending order—within which Kardec distinguished ten subcategories. Such precision demonstrated a schoolmasterish interest in structuring knowledge; the spirits, like natural objects, had to be classified and labeled.

Allan Kardek, who adopted henceforth his Druidic name, completed his arduous task in 1857 and sought a publisher. No firm in Paris would touch the project, so Kardec without hesitation took on himself the cost of publication and distribution. The edition quickly sold out, but even he could hardly have anticipated that the *Book of Spirits* would go through fifty editions during the next fifty years, or that new printings would continue to appear as recently as the 1970s in such exotic places as Brazil and Boston. Kardec accumulated substantial royalties from this and succeeding works—notably the *Book of Mediums*, an elaborate manual for the guidance of aspiring intermediaries with the spirit world. Well before he died in 1869, Kardec had earned enough from his writings to become a prosperous property owner; he built six town houses on the avenue de Ségur in Paris.

But financial gain was neither Kardec's principal concern nor the most important dividend of his new career. Rather, that dividend was his dramatic transmutation from obscure pedant into guru of a rapidly growing cult. One of his biographers suggests that Kardec suddenly discovered in himself an unsuspected talent as entrepreneur and publicist—that he became a master of *propagande à l'américaine.*" That judgment might seem to imply that Kardec was essentially a charlatan, or a French equivalent of P. T. Barnum. Such a conclusion would surely be excessive: all the evidence suggests that Kardec believed in what he was doing, perhaps through a kind of self-hypnosis. But even though the Barnum parallel is unjust, Kardec's remarkable success as cult leader owed something to his flair for publicity and persuasion.

Within months after the *Book of Spirits* appeared, Kardec set out to create an organized movement. He founded a monthly journal called the *Revue Spirite*, designed to spread the word and to attract new believers. Once again, he financed the journal personally and served as its editor; once again, its content was derived mainly from the spirits themselves, who continued to supply him with messages from beyond. Kardec next formed the Parisian Society of Spirit Studies, duly legalized by authorization of the Prefect of Police. Its members met at first in his apartment on the rue des Martyrs, but growing numbers soon forced a move to more spacious quarters. The Society eventually settled in at 59 rue Sainte-Anne, and the Kardecs took up residence in an adjoining apartment. Kardec delivered weekly lectures to the faithful; his status as guru discouraged questions and challenges from the membership. The movement spread from Paris to the provinces; from 1860 onward, Kardec made annual forays of several weeks to various provincial cities, speaking to audiences that reached five or six hundred. One might expect such crowd response to transform the dry-as-dust schoolmaster into a highly emotional revivalist, spurred by the faithful into charismatic transports. But no such change occurred in Allan Kardec; he retained the serious didactic tone of the pedagogue concerned to educate rather than to arouse his listeners. Spiritism was to him, after all, a science, not a religion. He instructed his followers to gather in small groups and, after reading a passage from the *Book of Spirits*, to engage in serious discussion of the text.

Kardec's associates claimed, shortly after his death, that he had converted 600,000 Frenchmen to spiritism. He himself spoke of an even wider following; he was in regular contact, he said, with a thousand centers of the movement throughout the entire world. Certainly the success of his evangelism was impressive; hundreds of letters weekly poured into the Society's headquarters, where Madame Kardec coped with the flood as the movement's voluntary secretary. Although Kardec's converts were impressed by spiritism's claim to a scientific base, most of them sought and found something more profound than that: the consolations of a quasi-religious faith. Kardec's doctrine offered them not only a glimpse into the nonmaterial recesses of the universe, but also an absolute assurance that life would continue after death, and that God would guide mankind in a continuous advance toward perfection. An essential element in Kardec's system was reincarnation; the soul whose corporeal envelope was the body survived the death of that envelope, and became for a time an "errant" spirit, wandering freely through the universe until assigned by God to a newborn infant. This process, Kardec learned from his spirit-informers, would continue through several or many lifetimes, until the spirit reached the state of purity and could retire with the status of angel. Furthermore, the process was destined to be one-way—always progressive, never regressive. True, there might be temporary setbacks: a spirit that had misbehaved might be punished by being reassigned to a less virtuous individual; but God's essential purpose was not to punish but to test. Each spirit was required to work its way up in the hierarchy to the state of purity; all were assured of eventually reaching that beatific goal, but some would get there more rapidly than others. Spirits, after all, were endowed with free will; it was their responsibility to avoid actions that would slow the process. God's testing system expected each indwelling spirit to provide wise guidance while in corporeal form. But some spirits were ignorant, frivolous, mischievous, or malevolent; their faults had to be overcome by repeated incarnations, each one a new test and a new opportunity. Spirits were not sexually differentiated; they could be reincarnated alternately in male and female bodies. But reincarnation in animal form could not occur; animals too had souls that survived as spirits, but on a lower plane than those of humans.

This optimistic prognosis, which defined all spirits as equal at the beginning and at the end of the race, offered hope to the faithful but also explained why living beings differed in fortunes or morality. Heartening also was the assurance of Kardec's spirit informers that each individual was blessed not only with a soul (the indwelling spirit) but with an *Esprit protecteur* or guardian angel. These special spirits were capable of intervening at crucial moments to help the individual over an obstacle or to rescue him from danger. Presumably it was this aspect of the doctrine that led Kardec's successors to claim Eugène Sue as one of the three great forerunners of spiritism. Sue's novels specialized in guardian angels, and suggested a belief in reincarnation.

Kardec's insistence that spiritism was a science led him to provide the doctrine with a scientific vocabulary. He drew heavily on the language of magnetism and somnambulism (hypnosis), and even asserted in the *Book of Spirits* that spiritism and magnetism were, "so to speak, one and the same." The special talents required of a medium, he declared, were those of expert magnetizers who could evoke a hypnotic state. To confound skeptics, he suggested analogies between spiritism and electricity. Electricity was known to exist even though it could not be seen; why not likewise the spirit world? Kardec borrowed also from magnetism the idea of a universal fluid that suffused the universe and served as a means of rapid transmission and instant communication for the spirits. In addition, he also provided each spirit with a *périsprit*—a filmy, almost transparent cloak within which the spirit resided after leaving the body. The claim to scientific status was further buttressed by the sober language and the systematic structure of Kardec's writings and lectures; he classified spirits as a botanist would classify plants.

Kardec insisted, however, that his new science in no way challenged the existence of God; rather, it provided scientific confirmation of God's existence. The real enemy, he contended, was materialism—the narrow insistence that nothing existed beyond the visible and tangible world. His relationship with Christianity was more complex. During his lifetime he avoided any challenge to religious institutions or beliefs, but his spirit-informers warned him that the Roman church would soon unleash a merciless campaign of persecution to destroy spiritism. The church, however, would destroy itself in this holy war, and the time was near when Kardek would proclaim spiritism as the only truly Christian tradition. Two or three generations would suffice to enlighten all doubters and to inaugurate the age of spiritism. "It is Christianity that opens the way, and on which spiritism is based."

As for the skeptics who rejected the existence of spirits and who asked for proof of that existence, Kardec replied impatiently that there was abundant proof. It was provided by direct observation, not a resort to faith; he himself and thousands of others had experienced their presence, had heard and tested the validity of the messages from the other world. If certain aspects remained mysterious, the same had been true of other natural phenomena before science had advanced far enough to explain them. Kardec warned that charlatans were continually at work seeking to profit by the gullibility of the public; he admitted too that the spirits could not always be trusted to give true answers or provide sound advice, for the "impure" spirits often amused themselves by teasing or misleading their mediums.

Kardec himself never claimed to possess the qualities of a medium; he depended on those endowed with the gift, most of whom were women. He did, however, provide detailed instruction on how to be a medium, derived from his spirit-informers. By the 1860s mediumistic techniques had advanced enormously; the primitive methods of table-turning and tapping by codes had been largely replaced by various forms of spirit-writing and by the appearance of "visual" and "auditory" mediums. Indeed, mediumship had become so specialized that Kardec could describe a new breed of "historian mediums" with a special talent for evoking historical knowledge even when they possessed no such learning themselves. Kardec provided in his *Book of Mediums* a classic example of his own experience with a *medium voyant*:

> One evening we were present at a performance of the opera "Oberon" with a very good visual medium. There was a rather large number of empty seats in the hall, but many of these were occupied by Spirits who seemed to be participating in the spectacle; some drew near certain spectators and appeared to be listening to their conversation. On the stage things were different; several jovial Spirits hovered behind the performers and amused themselves by imitating their gestures in grotesque fashion; others, more serious, seemed to inspire the singers with greater energy. One of them hovered constantly about a leading female singer; we suspected him of somewhat frivolous intentions. Having summoned him after the curtain fell, he came to our seats and reproached us rather severely for our hasty judgment. I am not what you think, he said; I am her guide and *Esprit protecteur*; I am assigned to direct her. After several minutes of very serious conversation, he left us, saying: Farewell; she is in her dressing room; I must go to watch over her. We then evoked the Spirit of Weber, the opera's composer, and asked him what he thought of the performance of his work. "It's not too bad," he said, "but it's flabby; the actors sing, but

that's all; they lack inspiration. Wait," he added, "I'm going to try to provide them with a bit of sacred fire." Then we saw him on the stage, hovering above the actors; an effluvium seemed to emanate from him and to spread about them; at that moment we could see an obvious surge of energy.

Kardec's ambition was breathtaking in its scope. He intended not only to convert all mankind to the science of spiritism, but also to prepare a new and better world governed by a universal moral law. It was a program rooted in the teachings of his boyhood master Pestalozzi and in his own youthful dreams of reforming the world. The ethical principles that he professed would be hard to fault (except, perhaps, for his insistence on the sacred right of property ownership). He was a feminist, advocating absolute equality of rights (though different aptitudes) for men and women. He was a pacifist, denouncing war and predicting a time when it would be outlawed. He exalted the idea of human brotherhood, with the Golden Rule as its foundation. He preached an end to "the prejudices of sects, castes, and colors."

The modest fortune that he amassed as leader of spiritism changed his life-style very little. He and his wife continued their spartan habits, working long hours and living in their cramped quarters on the rue Sainte-Anne. In 1869, at the age of sixty-five, Kardec decided at last to take semiretirement and to move to one of the six new town houses he had built on the avenue de Ségur. But on the eve of moving day, as he was completing copy for the next issue of the *Revue Spirite*, a massive heart attack struck him down. His will provided that on the death of his widow, his estate would be used to finance the creation of a Spirite Institute. (As it turned out, distant heirs challenged and managed to break the will.)

Kardec was buried without benefit of clergy in Montmartre cemetery, until Madame Kardec could prepare a proper tomb in Père

Lachaise. There his body was finally put to rest in 1870, beneath a massive imitation of a Breton dolmen—three massive slabs of granite, like the tombs of the ancient Druids whom he claimed as his ancestors. Among the speakers at the ceremony was the spirit of Allan Kardec, whose words were transmitted through a medium. Almost daily from that time until our own, the tomb has been literally buried under floral offerings; clusters of faithful devotees from far-flung lands arrive daily to commune with the master's spirit and to perform the mystic rite of touching his bust. Spiritism, despite his expectations, has not taken over the world, nor has a universal moral law altered the conduct of men. Yet Hippolyte Rivail, alias Allan Kardec, has achieved the status of talisman, and thus a degree of immortality.

Mme Clémence ROYER.

4

Clémence Royer
Polymath out of Season

Clémence Royer was born of an irregular union; she had little formal schooling; she never married, but bore a son; she died in relative poverty. She lectured, wrote, and published doggedly for forty years, yet she never held a salaried appointment on a university faculty or in a research institute. Charles Darwin, whose classic work *The Origin of Species* was translated into French by Madame Royer, called her "one of the cleverest and oddest women in Europe." Ernest Renan is said to have described her as "almost a man of genius."

The burgeoning of interest in women's history in recent years has begun the resurrection of Clémence Royer from the pit of obscurity into which she had fallen. Only a decade ago, a reader browsing through the Bibliothèque Nationale's printed catalogue would have been startled to find five full pages devoted to works by Madame Royer—thirty-two titles in all. True, many of these items were offprints of periodical articles which she persistently deposited in the library. Nevertheless, the collection represents an impressive body of work spread over a striking variety of scholarly fields. Such a bibliography in our time would surely suffice to justify an appointment to a chair in a good university, perhaps even to the Sorbonne. How could so learned a scholar have failed to achieve academic success? And how could her name have faded so quickly from the historical record?

At least part of the answer, of course, is that France in the nineteenth century was not a congenial place for women scholars. Those Frenchwomen who had intellectual pretensions were usually disparaged as *bas-bleus* (bluestockings), and were often regarded as figures of fun. A few women attained distinction in literature, though they often found it politic to adopt masculine *noms de plume*. Occasionally one strayed into a more esoteric field—for example, the mathematician Sophie Germain. But the mores of the time discouraged such ventures, and France's institutional structures reinforced these mores. The *baccalauréat* examination, which controlled access to higher education and professional careers, was closed to women until the 1870s, and even then was pushed ajar only slowly. One ambitious girl named Julie Daubié, who studied at home with her brothers while they attended a *lycée,* showed up for the examination in 1861 and passed with honors, but the baffled authorities denied her the diploma that would have allowed her to enter the university. From the 1880s onward, a few women managed to earn degrees in medicine or law, though elementary teaching was a more acceptable goal for those with ambition and talent. As late as 1914, only 10 per cent of French university students were women; and only in 1906 (four years after Clémence Royer's death) did a woman—the Nobel laureate Marie Curie—become a Sorbonne professor.

For a woman of scholarly bent like Clémence Royer, this state of affairs was both frustrating and infuriating. She believed that she measured up mentally to the men of her generation, and she was not shy about demanding her rights. She was determined to gain recognition in the scholarly world despite the formidable institutional roadblocks. Her failure to accomplish that goal embittered her spirit: "All my life," she wrote in her last will and testament, "I have suffered for having been a woman." If she had received recognition, perhaps she would have mellowed into a less abrasive and eccentric character. Still, abrasiveness and eccentricity do sometimes survive academic success.

Augustine-Clémence Audouard was born in Nantes in 1830, and became Clémence Royer seven years later when her parents got around to marrying. Royer *père* was an army officer whose loyalty to the Bourbon dynasty led him to resign his commission in 1830 and to take part in a plot to restore the "legitimate" king. When the conspiracy was exposed, he took his family into Swiss and German exile for several years. On their return, the Royers settled in Le Mans and placed their young daughter in a Catholic school for children of legitimist parents. Two years of intense indoctrination there turned the young teenager into a mystic and a zealot. When her father proposed to broaden her education by taking her to a theater, Clémence reacted with righteous horror; to ward off this devilish suggestion, she crossed herself ostentatiously. Her outraged father slapped her smartly, and withdrew her from the nuns' care. So ended her formal education.

The family moved to Paris in the 1840s, but constant domestic quarrels led finally to a formal separation; Clémence remained with her mother. The revolution of 1848 converted her into a republican, but not into a social democrat. Many years later, questioned by a socialist acquaintance about her memories of the bloody clash in June 1848 "inspired by misery and hunger," she replied brusquely: "There were no riots caused by misery and hunger." She set out to educate herself by auditing courses at the Sorbonne, the Collège de France, and especially at the Conservatoire des Arts et Métiers, where experts in technology and science lectured to popular audiences. For a few months she taught French and piano at a school in Wales, where she learned English. Somewhere en route she lost her religious faith; she became a lifetime freethinker and a harsh critic of organized religion. On her return to Paris her mother urged her to marry, but there too she had made up her mind: never, she said, would she engage in that "dangerous lottery." To escape the pressure she departed alone for Switzerland, shadowed by her mother's suspicion that she had gone mad. A new stage in her self-education now began. For two years she lived with a peasant family in a mountain village above Lausanne, reading voraciously from the holdings of a circulating library; then in 1857 she moved to Lausanne itself, and settled into the university library there.

Like most autodidacts, she read with more energy than discipline; but her interests were impressively broad, and they converged on a common center. She focused especially on what would now be called the social sciences, the natural sciences, and philosophy broadly conceived. Impatient to teach but lacking any formal credentials, she launched forth on her own; in 1858 she announced a course of lectures on logic open to the ladies of Lausanne. Its success was sufficiently encouraging to lead to a more ambitious project in 1859–60: a course of forty lectures entitled "Introduction to the Philosophy of Women," consisting of ten lectures each on metaphysics, psychology, natural philosophy, and "the philosophy of humanity." The fact that she attracted fifty women for so rich a diet speaks well for the intellectual interests of Swiss women of that time, and suggests her own self-confidence as a newly fledged scholar. Her fifty listeners stayed with her faithfully through the first three segments of the course, but all except three fled in panic when she undertook to explain and defend the evolutionary doctrines of Lamarck. Such ideas upset their orthodox religious views about the creation.

Soon after her arrival in Lausanne Clémence met the French historian and political economist Pascal Duprat, a republican exile who was currently teaching at the university. Duprat had been an elected representative in the French Parliament from 1848 to 1851; Napoleon's coup d'état had driven him abroad. For Clémence he became a kind of informal counselor whose advice she readily accepted. In response to his urging, she wrote a didactic novel, eventually published in Brussels, that portrayed a new form of marriage based on mutual affection, a free union of partners, and filiation through the maternal side. Progress toward this new age of freedom, she believed, was blocked by the Roman church and especially by the Jesuits who, in her opinion, preached morality but lived a lie. Not surprisingly, the novel was promptly placed on the Index alongside the writings of another Jesuit-hater, Eugène Sue; but unlike Sue's work her book found few readers.

Far more effective in building up her reputation was her venture into economics, again on Duprat's advice. In 1860 she entered a competition sponsored by one of the Swiss learned academies on the origins, purposes, and possible improvement of systems of taxation. Her essay was ranked third, with the noted pamphleteer P.J. Proudhon carrying off the top honors. In this essay she proposed, well in advance of its time, a proportional and progressive income tax— but only as a temporary device until "excessive inequality" among citizens had been corrected. She was evidently unaware that Karl Marx and Friedrich Engels had made a similar proposal in their *Communist Manifesto*. She also advocated a heavy tax on landed property, and even suggested that it be publicly owned; but she opposed taxing "productive capital" which was used for society's good. More unorthodox were her ideas about the role of women in the social order. Women, she argued, should be recognized as having a profession, whether managing the home or working outside it; they should pay the tax or license fee *(patente)* authorizing them to carry on that profession. But once they became mothers they should be freed of that tax, for the task of bringing up useful new citizens was a sufficient contribution to society. "Motherhood," she declared, "is women's equivalent of military service."

Over the years, taxation was to remain one of Madame Royer's special interests; she assiduously attended and spoke at congresses on the subject. But she gained far more attention when she shifted from the arid realm of economics to the more controversial arena of natural history. Charles Darwin's *Origin of Species* had appeared in 1859, and Madame Royer soon published a French translation of that seminal work, with a long and highly personal introductory essay. Her purpose was to challenge the religious establishment and to show that Darwin's research confirmed Lamarck's evolutionary theory of the inheritance of acquired characteristics—a theory which she herself had seized upon with enthusiasm and was eager to prove. Although she misread Darwin on the Lamarck issue, and probably misled those French readers who relied on her commentary, she did win the notice of the French scientific community for the first time. Her translation had "immense repercussions," if we are to believe the leading French encyclopedia of the time.

In fact, Madame Royer's introduction went well beyond the content of The *Origin of Species*, for she detected implications that Darwin and his popularizers would not draw until some years later. She put forward what was probably the first important expression of the doctrine that later came to be called social Darwinism: the idea that the struggle for existence operated not only in the animal world but also in the human realm, and not only among individuals but also among classes and races of men. The concept of natural selection, she contended, was merely a broadening out of Malthus's law: species multiply more rapidly than the means for their subsistence, and therefore the strongest and best adapted survive. But Darwin's law, she said, unlike that of Malthus, was not brutal but "providential"; it offered a guarantee of continuing progress, if only political and religious leaders would learn its lesson. The lesson was that both laws and morals must be changed; the time had come to sweep away "that imprudent and blind charity which our Christian era has always held up as the ideal of social virtue, and which democracies would like to transform into a kind of obligatory brotherhood. That doctrine leads to sacrificing the strong to the weak, the good to the bad, the well-endowed to those who are vice-ridden and sickly." Society, she asserted, is wrongly expected to lavish care on its degenerate members, but does nothing to nurture merit, talent, and virtue. On the contrary: the most robust and intelligent specimens are decimated in wars and dangerous occupations, leaving procreation to the old and sickly.

The root of the problem, Madame Royer declared, was the "futile and harmful" idea of equality. "Men are unequal by nature: that is the essential starting-point." So too with races: "Nothing is more obvious than the inequalities of various human races; nothing is more marked than these inequalities among the diverse individuals of the same race. Nothing allows us to doubt that the superior races are destined to replace the inferior ones, not to mix with them so as to lower the average level of the species." The theory of natural selection, she continued, teaches us to reject both the idea of absolute equality and that of a rigid caste society. The lesson in the political realm is the need for a regime of the most unlimited individual liberty, involving free competition and the right of free association. Her profession of faith in racist and libertarian principles ended in a broadside of invective against all potential critics: Darwin's book "will necessarily be opposed by all the brahmins, wise men, destours (Parsee high priests), levites, bonzes, priests and tricksters of all times and countries, not even omitting the sad preachers of evangelical protestantism in their white cravats and black frock-coats."

Madame Royer's rejection of the idea of equality did not extend, however, to relationships between the sexes. She accepted Darwin's idea that evolution had worked to make men mentally superior to women, but refused to follow him in his belief that the mental gap was now too great ever to be closed. For Clémence, the inferiority of women stemmed mainly from the abuse of male authority, and that could be corrected. Education was the secret; through that agency, equality (or at least equivalence) between the sexes could be achieved. She also thought that over time, the process of evolution itself could be modified. Heretofore, it had worked to make men more intelligent and women more beautiful; with reformed mores, the qualities of the two sexes would gradually converge.

In some of her subsequent writings, Madame Royer diverged somewhat from her ultralibertarian creed. She still held that the state should get off the backs of adult citizens, but demanded sweeping state action on behalf of children "from birth to adulthood." All children of workers should be provided free of charge with social services and education: "nurseries, shelters, primary schools, professional-training schools." No increase in taxes would be needed. "It would suffice to build schools instead of barracks, to buy books in place of cannons, and to replace every priest with a teacher." In short, "nothing from the state for the adult, everything for the child." Had she, then, evolved into the role of social reformer, moved by the kind of compassion which she condemned in Christians and democrats? Probably not; her interest in nurturing children was always expressed in instrumental terms, as a technique for producing more efficient and self-reliant citizens.

By the mid-1860s Clémence Royer had achieved a considerable reputation that brought her invitations to lecture in Belgium, Germany, Italy, and even occasionally in France. In 1865 a French visitor to Turin heard her lecture on Darwin in the auditorium of the *lycée* there and recorded his highly favorable impression. "Is it not strange," he wrote, "to find Darwin's ideas on the lips of a woman, a young woman at that? Mademoiselle Clémence Royer is a person aged twenty-five to thirty years [actually thirty-five], large, well-built, with an intelligent face; she speaks easily in a sonorous voice, lectures for a full hour without notes, holding forth on the weightiest questions of geology and anthropology. I thought I was dreaming." Much less admiring was the judgment of the young writer Juliette Lamber (later Juliette Adam), who met Clémence at a literary salon during one of Clémence's brief visits to Paris. Juliette described Clémence, in later retrospect, as "a person of masculine appearance, without social graces, who spoke loudly and with authority"; sparks flew at once, catty and cutting remarks were exchanged, and Juliette thenceforth always referred to Clémence as "my enemy."

Meanwhile Clémence had encountered love for the first and only time in her life. She had known Pascal Duprat since 1858, but it was not until 1865, when they met again at a scholarly congress in Geneva, that they talked of their future and agreed to live together in what was then called a free union. Duprat's freedom of action was somewhat hampered by the fact that he had a wife and daughter, who lived with him intermittently during his years of exile. The couple's relationship was stormy, however; Madame Duprat complained that her husband was a poor provider, and finally returned to Paris where influential friends persuaded Napoleon III's bureaucrats to grant her a kind of disguised pension in the form of permission to operate a *bureau de tabac*. Duprat was ready therefore to embark on a new extra-legal relationship, and that suited Clémence's belief in a new morality. They settled together in northern Italy, where a son was born in 1866. Clémence and her child went back to Paris in 1869, and were joined by Duprat a year later when the fall of the Empire ended his exile. He was elected to Parliament in 1871 and continued to sit as deputy for the next ten years; but for Clémence he was an albatross rather than a source of support. Contantly saddled with debts, unlucky in his business ventures, a marginal man in politics, he leaned on Clémence to keep him out of the grip of his creditors. She protected him by leasing their apartment in her name, so that his meager possessions could not be seized for debt; he contributed only sporadically to their household expenses. In 1881 he lost his seat in Parliament, but his political allies got him an appointment as France's minister to Chile. Returning in 1885 to try his luck again in the elections, he was struck down en route by a heart attack. Clémence had earlier forsworn the "dangerous lottery" of marriage, but what she got instead was scarcely better. She later lamented that in linking her fate to Duprat's, "I married misery, and I endured it for twenty years." Yet she also remembered him as "the only love of my life," and excused his financial ineptitude by blaming his wife and daughter for their badgering demands.

From the time of her return to Paris in 1869, Clémence Royer embarked on a thirty-year campaign to achieve recognition in the city's intellectual world. The range of her scholarly interests, already impressive, became even broader; she wrote and lectured on social, economic, political, philosophical, biological, and anthropological questions. Her publications ranged from "Funeral Rites in Prehistoric Epochs" to "Public Assistance in France since 1789," from "The History of Heaven" to "The Life and Doctrine of Zoroaster," from "Attraction and Gravitation According to Newton" to "The Unknowable." She contributed regularly to a number of scholarly periodicals, and was admitted to membership in the new Société d'Anthropologie de Paris, which became her real scholarly home. The Société not only published many of her papers in its journal, but gave her a forum where she could engage in debate with her male colleagues. She used the opportunity with tireless energy; the Société's president reported at her funeral that she had spoken 132 times in the course of its sessions. She concluded that anthropology was the queen of the sciences; it was congenial to her encyclopedic intellectual interests, and besides it gave her formal recognition.

Nevertheless, real acceptance by the intellectual establishment of Paris continued to elude her. Since she lacked access to the most prestigious learned societies, she founded her own: the Société des études philosophiques et morales, open to both sexes. But it tended to attract cranks and fanatics—"socialist utopians and spiritist dreamers," she called them—so she soon abandoned the Société. On every occasion, she entered prize competitions announced by the Académie des Sciences Morales et Politiques, but rarely with success. She sought lecture platforms for her public courses, but was often denied them—sometimes by the Prefecture of Police, again by the authorities of the Sorbonne. Her major handicap was of course that she was a woman without scholarly credentials, but her assertive and abrasive personality surely added to her difficulties. To an acquaintance she made this candid admission: "I don't know how to talk to crowds; instead of flattering them, I'm always tempted to rub them the wrong way, to tell them that they are Panurge's flock, a flock of donkeys and wolves rather than sheep." When the old utopian socialist Victor Considerant tried to offer her advice on how to make a better impression on her listeners, she replied angrily: "It seems that only male professors have the right to be ugly and to dress as they like, while paying more attention to what a woman wears than to the truth of what she says," Her stiff-necked independence of mind got her into trouble with Darwin, among others; when she ignored his revisions in a later edition of *The Origin of Species*, he sought out another translator. Karl Marx rejected her as a prospective translator of *Das Kapital*, but for other reasons; her introduction to Darwin showed, he said, that she was a bourgeoise.

Advancing age brought Madame Royer a mixed reward: the pains of poverty, the pleasures of long deferred recognition. She had always lived rather precariously: her writings produced little income, and her lecture courses lacked an institutional base. In 1888 she was reduced to petitioning the government for the right to open a *bureau de tabac*—an action that must have caused her considerable mental anguish. The police report appended to this request estimated that she earned about 1200 francs a year from her writings, in addition to which she received an annual grant of 800 to 1200 francs from the Ministry of Public Instruction. Almost half of her total income went for the rental of a succession of small and cheap apartments; little margin was left for other basic expenses. The bureaucracy evidently failed to act on the tobacco shop permit. Perhaps it was her sense of grievance at this neglect that led her to support the campaign of General Boulanger, who proposed at the end of the 1880s to transform the Third Republic into an authoritarian regime. At any rate, in 1892 she was admitted to a new hospice for elderly and indigent writers and printers in the suburb of Neuilly. This hospice, established by the English-born philanthropist William Galignani, provided shelter for a hundred oldsters lucky enough to gain admission. There she remained for ten years, until her death in 1902 at the age of seventy-five. She continued her compulsive writing, despite the multiple ailments of old age; "I am dying piece by piece," she complained to a friend. She enjoyed the satisfaction, however, of seeing her son, René Duprat, graduate from the elite École Polytechnique and receive an army commission—a somewhat uncertain consolation in light of her pacifist views.

More heartening, however, was her adoption in the 1890s as a kind of *maitresse à penser* by a small but fervent coterie of second-level Parisian intellectuals, and as a symbolic standard-bearer by some of the leading feminists of the time. Some of her male admirers were veterans of the learned society which she had founded in 1880, and had remained loyal when she gave up active leadership of that organization. They greeted her magnum opus in 1900—*Natura rerum: la constitution du monde*, a massive and highly philosophical compendium of her views on the universe, based on the concept of a dynamic "fluid atom"—as a work of almost unmatched genius. Some of them took to describing her as "the French Newton," and recalled Ernest Renan's reference to her as "almost a man of genius." Such adulation, though late in arriving, was balm to her spirit.

More striking still was her adoption by the feminists. Her relations with the activists in the women's movement had always been somewhat ambiguous. She had helped Maria Deraismes start a feminist journal toward the end of the Second Empire, and she had regularly attended European feminist congresses; but she had been more fellow-traveler than activist. Her ideas of woman's role were a bit quirky; she opposed the vote for women on the ground that they were still too much subject to clerical influence to be trusted with the ballot. Furthermore, she asked, why should women "demand" rights which they already possessed; all they had to do was to assert them. Women, she insisted, were free to do anything they wished except to be useless parasites. Her only sign of militancy was to reject the title Mademoiselle; when she received letters so addressed, they were returned unopened to the sender. "Madame Royer" or "Clémence Royer" were the names she always chose—though on one exceptional occasion she did record herself as "Madame Veuve Duprat."

In 1892, two of the leading feminist organizations chose Clémence as a symbolic heroine. They presented her candidacy, unsuccessfully, to the all-male Académie des Sciences Morales et Politiques. A year later they tried to persuade her to run for the Chamber of Deputies; she refused. She met them halfway, however, by helping to organize France's first mixed Masonic lodge (1893), and by contributing regularly to *La Fronde*, Marguerite Durand's daily newspaper by and for women. In 1897 the feminists staged an impressive banquet in her honor; three hundred admirers attended and loaded her with encomiums. In 1900 they persuaded the government to award her the Legion of Honor. Her last years, then, were not devoid of satisfaction. There were many laudatory speeches in 1902 at her funeral services in the Neuilly cemetery, where three hundred fifty of her faithful friends gathered for a last tribute. Some of them had proposed that her brain be removed for scientific study, but she had forestalled this by a specific clause in her will. Her admirers continued to exalt her memory; in 1930, to celebrate the centennial of her birth, they organized a commemorative session at the Sorbonne, where in her lifetime she had been denied the use of a classroom. One disciple even proposed the establishent of a Clémence Royer University to celebrate the breadth of her learning.

Clémence Royer's proper place in the intellectual life of nineteenth-century Paris is not easy to assess. She herself never lost faith in her own genius; she died convinced that posterity would recognize her greatness at last. In a codicil to her will, she named a publication committee of twenty-four distinguished citizens to supervise new editions of her works and to publish the mass of manuscripts she left behind; she estimated that these would fill ten volumes. The proceeds from this enterprise she assigned to her son René (who in fact survived her by only a few months), and, in case of his death, to a new society for the propagation of her theory of *dynamisme atomique*. No such society was ever established; the publications committee never met; no new editions appeared, and the unpublished manuscripts vanished without a trace.

Few of Madame Royer's male contemporaries were such tireless workers, and in scholarly ability and achievement she measured up to most of them. She had an ingenious and questioning mind, and an astounding breadth of interests. She was often self-righteous, and rarely showed much compassion for those less fortunate or less intelligent. She can fairly be accused of contradicting herself at times. If she possessed what the French call *un caractère pas facile*, that was surely the product in part of her lifetime of frustration. The interest that persists in the record of her life stems mainly from the way an isolated woman in nineteenth-century France could buck the system and achieve at least marginal success. With enormous energy and unflagging determination, she asserted her right to learn and teach, to speak and write, despite all efforts by the establishment to ignore her or to keep her down. If she had lived in our day, with access to formal education and to a university chair, she might have become a respected and influential member of the recognized intellectual élite. On the other hand, such a destiny might make her life seem less interesting in retrospect. Lonely fighters are often more intriguing than successful conformists.

5

Juliette Adam
Egeria of the Republic

In the legends that cluster about the founding of ancient Rome, a beautiful water nymph named Egeria played an important role. King Numa, seeking advice on the building of his new state, is supposed to have ventured into the forest by night to consult Egeria on these weighty questions. Many centuries later, the founders of the French Third Republic found their own Egeria in Madame Edmond Adam (née Juliette Lambert). Léon Gambetta, the leading statesman of the nascent republic, addressed her as "ma belle Egérie," a title that she relished. Some malicious critics alleged that she really wished to be known as the uncrowned queen of the republic; and late in life she accepted with pleasure the label "la Grande Française."

Juliette Lambert, like so many notable Parisians, came out of the provinces to undertake the conquest of Paris. Born in the small Picard town of Chauny in 1836, she spent her early years in conditions that have overtones of a modern soap opera. Rejected by her mother, she was raised by her grandparents and then, in adolescence, spent part of each year with her doctor father. Family gatherings were memorable, usually degenerating into shouting matches: grandfather worshipped Napoleon, grandmother was a monarchist, three great-aunts professed to be "liberals," and father was a utopian socialist. Juliette's grandparents sent her to a private Catholic girls' school and arranged to have her clandestinely baptized, infuriating her father who, like many doctors at the time, was a freethinker and ferocious anticlerical. It was her father who influenced the teenaged Juliette most strongly. Determined to save her from the reactionaries and the priests, he encouraged her to read Eugène Sue's *Wandering Jew* and the publications of the utopians; he taught her to admire the Greek spirit of classical balance and republican virtue, and to abandon the church in favor of a vague deism or pantheism. He urged her also to believe that a woman had the right and the duty to develop her intellectual capacities and to speak out on public issues. Such an upbringing was not a common experience for a young bourgeois Frenchwoman of her time.

Tradition, however, was not easily shaken off. At age sixteen she was affianced by her grandmother to a Parisian lawyer twice her age. She wept and protested, but in the end was forced to become Madame Alexis La Messine. The marriage proved to be a disaster; La Messine was evidently an unspeakable cad. Although a daughter was born after a year, the relationship disintegrated rapidly after the last installment of the dowry was paid. Juliette shuttled back and forth between Paris and Chauny; divorce being illegal at the time, the couple settled for a de facto separation. In 1861 La Messine was given a minor bureaucratic post in Algeria, where he remained until he died in 1867.

Juliette meanwhile had gradually shaken free of her provincial roots, and had settled with her young daughter in a cramped Paris apartment at 238 rue de Rivoli. Before long she began to attract some attention as an aspiring writer and a charming young ingenue on the fringes of Parisian society. Her first works went largely unnoticed, but in 1858 a long essay gave her an audience. It was a spirited and witty attack on P.J. Proudhon, who had just published a work that included his views on the proper role of women. Proudhon, a cranky political and social philosopher, was an uninhibited male chauvinist; Juliette was outraged by his attacks on George Sand and Marie d'Agoult, two women whom she admired deeply. For a young and unknown provincial to challenge a polemicist as formidable as Proudhon was indeed audacious. No editor would take on her manuscript, so her father offered her a thousand francs to subsidize its publication by a vanity press. In her *Idées anti-proud-honiennes sur l'amour, la femme et le mariage*, she ridiculed Proudhon and argued for the legal equality of men and women, the right of women to accede to all social roles, and the need to legalize divorce in order to free women from domestic slavery. Her book brought her immediate notoriety and lengthy commentaries in the press; it also won her admission to a leading literary salon, that of the Countess Marie d'Agoult.

The Countess was a major but somewhat unorthodox participant in the highly competitive social game-playing of Paris. Born in Germany where her father had emigrated during the Revolution, she had married an aging aristocrat whom she had deserted for a torrid affair with the romantic composer Franz Liszt. She lived with Liszt for several years and bore him three daughters, one of whom eventually married Richard Wagner. She had been actively involved in the political life of the Second Republic, and had written (under the pseudonym Daniel Stern) an insider's instant history of the 1848 revolution. The Countess had a large circle of influential friends, and was attracted to Juliette as a charming but somewhat naive young woman eager to become her protégée.

For several years Juliette adopted the role of admiring disciple and participated regularly in the d'Agoult salon. There she learned the techniques of this exacting trade: how to attract and retain the loyalty of the right people, how to entertain in style, how to stimulate conversation without dominating it. By 1864 she was ready to launch forth on her own; she inaugurated her own salon in her small apartment, devoted to discussion of literature, politics, and society gossip. The Countess, who evidently saw this as a disloyal act, broke off relations; Juliette professed shock, and later explained the breach by alleging that her "grande amie" had suffered a mental breakdown. But the break led to a new friendship with the famous novelist George Sand, who had been on bad terms with the Countess and therefore found Juliette a kindred spirit. Sand replaced the Countess as "ma grande amie" in Juliette's affections—though that friendship also cooled somewhat in later years, as Juliette began to transcend the protégée role.

Throughout the 1860s, as Juliette was making her way upward in social and literary circles, she was also developing a rather ambiguous relationship with a wealthy banker and republican politician named Edmond Adam. Twenty years her senior, Adam had met Juliette soon after her arrival in Paris, and had been bewitched by her beauty and charm. Juliette later claimed that she had thought him gray and unromantic at first, but had gradually come to like and admire him enough to think of marriage. The hitch of course was that she already had a husband: the egregious La Messine was still alive and could not be divorced. Gossips assumed that Juliette and Adam were engaged in an affair; indeed, if one is to believe the stories retailed by the Goncourt brothers, Adam found her almost more than he could handle. He allegedly complained to an acquaintance that if male bordellos existed, she would probably buy a season ticket. In 1867 came the news that La Messine had conveniently died, and a year later Juliette became Madame Edmond Adam. She rejoiced in that name, and used it now in place of her former *nom de plume* Juliette Lamber (shorn of the family name's final "t" for unexplained reasons).

Juliette and her new husband were, despite the difference in age, bound together by ties of deep affection and mutual respect. She quickly adopted and vigorously defended his political positions: Adam was an old-school republican of 1848 vintage, a rather austere exponent of middle-class ideals. Adam was respected by the republicans for his somewhat quixotic intransigence. He was so bitterly opposed to Napoleon III's Second Empire that he refused to join other republicans who sought to function as legal opposition to the regime; such activity, he held, would mean collaboration with the usurper. He brought some of his political friends into Juliette's salon. She in turn attracted a few writers and musicians whom she had met at the d'Agoult salon; but her circle remained small until her marriage put an end to her equivocal status as a grass widow with an uncertain social position. Adam brought her new respectability as well as ample resources; the couple moved to larger and more luxurious quarters at 23 Boulevard Poissonière in the heart of the city's commercial activity and social life, and the salon was relaunched with style. Some young republicans of the rising new generation (including, notably, their charismatic leader Gambetta) were attracted by Adam's status as an elder statesman, and were ensnared by Juliette's flattering attentions.

The fall of the Second Empire in September 1870 and the establishment of a provisional republic opened new horizons for Madame Adam. The republicans, still a minority in the country, closed ranks in an effort to convert the provisional regime into a permanent one. Both generations, the elders of the 1848 republic and the new more aggressive breed, were ready now to bury their differences. They felt the need for a congenial place where they could talk politics, plan strategy, and relax in friendly company. The new Adam apartment in the heart of Paris proved to be the natural locus. Juliette alone, of all the wives of leading republicans, was an experienced hand at managing a salon, while Adam's status as a republican of impeccable credentials and a man of means served as a magnet for ambitious politicians on the rise. But the success of the salon during the 1870s was essentially Juliette's. She was the only woman in this all-male club, and she had learned how to play the role of hostess to perfection. Warm-hearted and quick-witted, she was adept at sparking discussion or, when necessary, diverting arguments when they threatened to become incendiary. Serious political talk was the normal fare, but it was leavened by gourmet dinners and by such lighter entertainment as dominoes, chess, and card games. Throughout the decade the Adam salon remained the unofficial headquarters of the republican forces and, when schisms began to divide them, of the dominant faction known as Opportunists and headed by Gambetta.

This cozy arrangement was disrupted for a time by Edmond Adam's unexpected death in 1877, at the age of sixty-one. He had been almost as much a father-figure as a husband but her affection for him had been deep and had grown over the years. She was inconsolable for a time, and suspended her salon for a year. Her new widowed status opened a considerable range of possibilities, since she was still an attractive woman of forty-one with a fortune inherited from Adam. But she let it be known that Adam, a jealous man, had exacted from her a promise not to marry again for at least three years after his death—or so she said. Among the possible aspirants to her hand, there seems to have been only one whom she took seriously: Léon Gambetta. Her true relationship with the Great Tribune, as Gambetta was known in his day, remains the most difficult aspect of her life to penetrate with any certainty.

Undoubtedly there was a strong mutual attraction between them. Gambetta was a bachelor, a passionate womanizer and a natural charmer who had carried on affairs with a variety of partners over the years. His current paramour, Léonie Léon, was a divorcee with no claim to social status. Juliette's reputation, on the other hand, was above reproach; but she too possessed a passionate side that had lacked fulfillment during her first failed marriage and her rather cerebral relationship with Adam. Even before Adam's death—at least from 1873 onward—Gambetta had emerged as the ruling spirit of Juliette's salon, the star attraction who brought along a coterie of disciples and whose ebullient personality made him the center of every discussion. His rising national stature as the republicans' spokesman added to his glamor in Juliette's eyes; her adulation in turn warmed and flattered his Mediterranean spirit. Juliette, whose ambition for public recognition and private influence had grown with her worldly successes, aspired to become his most intimate political confidante; when she departed in 1874 for her annual long vacation on the Riviera, she begged Gambetta to keep her posted by letter on the Parisian political scene. He complied with remarkable readiness; despite his crushing schedule as party leader and member of Parliament, he took time to dash off a kind of daily journal covering behind-the-scenes politics and relating his own worries and successes. What sort of counsel he received in return from his "belle Egérie" is beyond our knowing, for her letters were later destroyed. We know only that she sent him bouquets of semitropical flowers, which he arranged and tended with sentimental care.

On most issues of public policy, Juliette and Gambetta seemed to be soulmates. Both were moved by a passionate patriotism, a refusal to accept the loss of Alsace-Lorraine as final, and a deep conviction that Bismarck was the irreconcilable enemy scheming to pick another fight with France. Both nourished an almost religious faith in the republican system and a determination to frustrate its enemies, the monarchists and the Church. They did argue at times over questions of political philosophy: for example, Juliette held that the republic should produce a ruling élite of superior men who would outshine those of any monarchy, while Gambetta rejected this elitism in favor of raising the level of the entire mass of citizens. And Madame Adam vehemently advocated an alliance with Russia against the common German enemy, while Gambetta remained skeptical and teased Juliette for her "Cossack" proclivities.

Was there a more intense electrical current between them, one that might easily have sparked love and marriage? Some of the phraseology of Gambetta's letters may suggest as much. "You will never know," he wrote, "to what degree pure egotism makes me love you to distraction." Or again: "I have so gradually become accustomed to living in your radiance that the rest of the world without you always seems cold, empty, devoid of light. I shall go on in the shadows until I find you again. I cast myself at your feet." Still, his fervency of expression may have reflected nothing more than his emotional southern temperament. Certainly none of his letters to Madame Adam approached the passionate intensity, the carnal urges of those he was writing at the same time to Léonie Léon. Yet his words may have suggested more than he intended to the more inhibited daughter of Picardy. She was accustomed to flattery, and thirsted for it; but no suitor had ever addressed her with Gambetta's intensity. Perhaps she read too much into his extravagant language. In any event, both parties remained scrupulously correct in their conduct so long as Adam was alive; neither would risk grave offense to a man they both respected.

That barrier, if it was one, was removed when Adam died in 1877. Did Gambetta then think seriously of a marriage based on mutual love and promising him the wealth and respectability that would further his political career? Juliette may well have seen the future thus, though she let it be known that she would postpone all thought of marriage during the three-year delay exacted by Adam. Those three years, however, brought a transformation of their relationship, which turned from warm to frigid. By 1879 Gambetta was no longer coming to her salon, and while they saw and corresponded with one another occasionally, their exchanges often degenerated into wrangles. Indeed, she turned to biting criticism of the great tribune during his last years, and after his death in 1882 she engaged in what might almost be called a posthumous vendetta against his memory. Her memoirs, written a quarter-century later, suggest that the freeze set in over differences about foreign policy. Gambetta, she alleged, had gradually abandoned the dream of *revanche*, and had become so dazzled by Bismarck's genius that he was ready for reconciliation with France's deadly enemy. She threatened that if Gambetta were to make a deal with Bismarck, "whose claws have torn out the heart of our nation, Alsace-Lorraine," she would leave Paris forever. Seeking in retrospect an explanation for Gambetta's "betrayal," she decided that he was not really French. His opportunism, she concluded, was rooted in the *combinazione* of his Italian heritage, whereas she herself had "the atavism of old France" in her blood. It is true that Gambetta was indeed seeking some kind of accommodation with Germany, and seriously considered a personal meeting with Bismarck; he brushed off Juliette's insistent advice that he seek a Russian alliance against the common enemy. France, he argued, must first recover her great-power status before issuing challenges to any rival.

Perhaps this policy conflict sufficed to produce the alienation that occurred toward 1880. Yet one suspects that more personal factors contributed as well. Juliette complained of Gambetta's continuing liaison with Léonie Léon, and did her best to break it up. Was jealousy her motive, or did she think it her duty to cure him of his bohemian ways so that he might aspire to the highest posts in the republic? One incident supports the latter hypothesis. When she learned that a notorious courtesan possessed some compromising letters from Gambetta and planned to sell them to the Bonapartists, she bought the letters herself and destroyed them. That episode may suggest that her concern for Gambetta's reputation was genuine and unselfish. Yet even if such was the case, Gambetta may have resented her interference in his private life. Besides, Adam's death probably led Gambetta to reassess his relationship with Juliette, and to adopt a more cautious line. Playing the flirtation game with a charming but unattainable lady was one thing, while the prospect of a lifetime commitment to that same strong-willed lady was quite another.

Adam's death and Gambetta's withdrawal from Juliette's salon altered its character. Most of Gambetta's followers dropped away, so that it lost its status as the Opportunists' political club. Political discussion remained on the agenda, but the salon now attracted a more varied and more conservative group of republicans, and eventually even occasional monarchists. Women, who had been rigorously excluded during the 1870s (except for Juliette), were now admitted. More and more, the activities broadened out to include literary readings, musical performances, debates, and even masked balls. Although the salon's character evolved, it retained much of its prestige in Parisian society. Some participants complained, however, that it was no longer confined to the governing élite, and even that some obscure social climbers were gaining access—as Guy de Maupassant described them, "those people who show up everywhere because they have been more or less introduced and because they own a black frock coat." Although Madame Adam still reigned as a leading hostess, her personal role had changed. She had begun as the skillful impresario of a galaxy of stars; now she herself had become the star, a more willful and domineering presence than before.

The salon, however, was not the only outlet for her energy. She persisted in her writing career, which indeed had never been interrupted for very long; she published some twenty novels or book-length essays between 1860 and 1900, along with a number of short plays. Her talent, though, was modest; her subjects quickly became dated. A more ambitious venture was her creation in 1879 of a bimonthly magazine called *La Nouvelle Revue*; she remained its editor and foreign affairs commentator for twenty years, and the Revue itself survived until 1940. In its pages she tirelessly preached her anti-German and pro-Russian line. Her stridency gave her recognition as one of the two leading French advocates of revenge, along with that professional patriot Edouard Déroulède. Bismarck himself is said to have exclaimed in anger, "Can no one silence this devil of a woman?"

Juliette's tireless activity and assertive temper might seem to suggest an inclination to join the feminist movement. Her father, after all, had been an advocate of women's rights, and Juliette's early writings gave promise that she would become a crusader. Yet she refused any formal involvement with the leading feminists of the time. She met the activist Maria Deraismes, and found her campaign interesting but not entirely congenial with her own views. She encountered the assertive polymath Clémence Royer a couple of times, but took an intense dislike to her, describing Royer in her memoirs as "my enemy." She summed up her own position on "the woman question" thus: "I continue to reject the simplistic formula of equality between men and women. I accept only the existence of complementary equivalences between them, the qualities of each partner in a balanced marriage combining to form the perfect social person." Such views would seem to make her a textbook example of what Karen Offen labels "relational feminism" as opposed to "individualist feminism"—the former variety stressing the male-female couple rather than the individual as the basic unit of society. But it did not inspire her to activism on behalf of her sex.

As editor of the *Nouvelle Revue*, Madame Adam collected a group of young protégés whose work was first published there: such figures as Paul Bourget, Pierre Loti, and Ernest and Léon Daudet. All of them belonged on the far right of the political spectrum, reflecting the fact that Juliette's own position had evolved sharply since the great days of the early republic. Although she claimed still to be a republican, she consorted now with some of the regime's most caustic critics and enemies, and she spoke more readily of authority than of liberty. The Dreyfus Affair found her an immediate and violent anti-Dreyfusard; she denounced the defenders of Dreyfus as subversives undermining national security. She warmly approved (except for its monarchist aspect) Charles Maurras's new-right movement the Action Française; she shared the "integral nationalism" preached by Maurras and Maurice Barrès. Juliette had already abandoned the anticlerical and pantheist beliefs she had inherited from her father; from the late 1880s onward she returned step by step to the Catholic faith of her childhood, proclaiming that France's soul was Catholic, and that only the atavistic Catholicism of Frenchmen could keep alive the sacred flame of *la revanche*. The distance she had traveled since the 1870s was breathtaking.

By the 1890s, however, her star was fading. Edmond de Goncourt, who encountered her now and again at dinner parties, liked to indulge both his snobbery and his misogyny at Juliette's expense. He and his cronies privately ridiculed her as a wrinkled old woman whose social *gaffes* were legendary and who remained at bottom "*une forte fermière de campagne.*" Yet on occasion he was impressed both by her amiability and by her ability to make sensible and precise conversation; she speaks, said Goncourt, like an *homme d'affaires*.

Juliette continued to hold court at her new residence, built to her order in 1882 and located on a private street which, with a regal touch, she chose to baptize the rue Juliette Lamber. City authorities made the name official in 1895; in that sense she became an enduring part of Parisian history. In most other ways, however, she was sliding toward obscurity. She had lost half her fortune in the collapse of the Union Générale bank in 1882, and had dissipated part of what remained in keeping *La Nouvelle Revue* afloat. She retired as its director in 1899, and gave up her foreign affairs column a few months later; but for several more years she continued to proclaim her unwavering anti-German and pro-Russian views in a miniature periodical created for that purpose. In 1904 she abandoned Paris for good, moving to her country house, a refurbished abbey at Gif, a few miles outside the city. In place of her salon, she staged country weekends for her Parisian friends, and spent her time writing several volumes of memoirs.

From this quiet suburban existence she was uprooted and energized by the outbreak of the Great War. Here at last was the promise of *la revanche*, for which she had worked so long and so ardently. Despite her age, she threw herself into wartime activities, organizing a society to provide warm clothing for the *poilus* (front-line soldiers), sponsoring a patriotic news sheet for the trenches, denouncing pacifists who sought to end the war. Her admirers accorded her a new accolade: "la Grande Française." When victory over the hated enemy came at last, she was given an honored place at the triumphal ceremonies. Premier Clemenceau is said to have sent his private car to carry her to Versailles where, in the Hall of Mirrors, she watched the humiliation of the German delegates. No doubt she saw it as the crowning moment in her long career, surpassing even the special prize of 10,000 francs awarded to her in 1927 by the Académie Française for her literary and patriotic accomplishments. She lived on at Gif, receiving a few intimate friends, then in 1931 retreating into the life of a recluse. She died in 1936, a month short of her hundredth birthday.

Not one but three memorials recall Juliette's career: the rue Juliette Lamber in Paris, the avenue Juliette Adam near her Riviera vacation home, and the bust of Madame Adam in the town hall of Gif. Yet few Frenchmen today would be able to identify the woman who accumulated these honors and bore this respected name. Several biographers—notably the able Egyptian scholar Saad Morcos—have sought to revivify her memory, but without visible success. For one thing, she lived too long, outlasting her historic moment. Furthermore, it would be difficult to show that she made any durable contribution to the well-being of the city and nation which she loved with such intensity. Indeed, her successes were probably the result of luck and chance more than the product of superior talents. She herself, concluding her memoirs on an uncharacteristically modest note, asked to be judged by the political and literary friendships she had made. A single sentiment, she declared, had dominated her life: her passionate love of *la patrie* and her unbreakable belief in the nation's resurgence. "My great-grandchildren," she added, "will again see France great, with a *grandeur* which their ancestor never doubted." Perhaps her spiritual heirs should include, among others, that apostle of the nation's grandeur, Charles de Gaulle.

6

Marquis de Morès
Adventurer in Four Worlds

Throughout his short life the Marquis de Morès continued to impress his contemporaries as a man quite out of the ordinary. His restless spirit carried him to the American Wild West, to the Indian jungle, to the remote interior of Indochina, and eventually to his death in the Sahara Desert. For a time in the 1890s it also brought him into a role in French politics, as an anti-Semitic rabble-rouser and protofascist. In his life span of thirty-eight years, there was enough adventure for a dozen normal lives.

Morès's paternal forebears had served and fought for the kings of Aragon and Sardinia and had been ennobled by them. His grandfather had moved to France in the early nineteenth century and had married a Frenchwoman also of high aristocratic birth. The future marquis was born in Paris in 1858, in a family mansion on the rue de Grenelle that would later house the Russian Embassy. Wealth as well as distinction was his birthright; the family possessed a villa in Cannes and a chateau near Dreux. The young man seemed destined for the usual life of the Proustian aristocracy—the social whirl of the Faubourg Saint-Germain, interspersed with vacations on the Riviera or in the country seats of family and friends. Or, as a more active alternative, there was the appeal of a military career, in the tradition of his ancestors.

It was the latter choice that attracted the young marquis-to-be. The romance of the sea drew him to the idea of a naval career, and he entered a preparatory school that specialized in training for the naval academy. But an attack of what was then called "brain fever" struck him down just as he was about to take the entrance examination, and forced a change of plan. He opted therefore for the army, and won admission to Saint-Cyr, the West Point of France, in 1877 (one year after Philippe Pétain, the future hero of Verdun and head of state at Vichy during World War II). An additional year at the cavalry school at Saumur honed his skills as rider and swordsman. He was then assigned to garrison duty near the German frontier. But even the excitement of two duels in which he is said to have killed his opponents failed to relieve the boredom of life in a garrison town. He abandoned his commission in 1881 and went off to Paris.

One of his motives for this sudden decision may have been a new romantic interest. While on leave in Paris he had met the attractive red-haired daughter of a wealthy New York banker, Louis A. von Hoffman. A whirlwind courtship ended successfully in marriage; the dowry was rumored to approach a million dollars. Morès and his new bride, Medora, sailed for New York in 1882, and the marquis settled into a position in Hoffman's banking house. But the sedentary life quickly palled; he was restless for action and adventure. A business acquaintance told him of vast open country in Dakota Territory, just made accessible by the Northern Pacific Railway. This acquaintance claimed to own several thousand acres there, including the buildings of an abandoned army cantonment, and he offered Morès an option on the property. Morès enthusiastically seized the opportunity—as he himself put it with characteristic modesty: "I pride myself on having a natural intuition. It takes me only a few seconds to understand a situation that other men have to puzzle over for hours"—and bought the option. In March 1883 he and his valet headed west, leaving his new bride behind. His destination was the Western Dakota Badlands near the Montana border, where the railway crossed the Little Missouri River.

What he found there was indeed raw frontier: a "town" of some two dozen souls, with a few settlers, squatters, and buffalo hunters scattered about on the open range. Worse still, he discovered that his option covered only some almost unusable army buildings, and none of the 8000 acres of range he had been promised. Always the optimist, he was not disheartened. He plunged at once into a hurricane of activity: laid out a town site for what was to become Medora (named for his wife), began the construction of a twenty-six room "chateau" on a bluff overlooking the site; bought a huge spread of range land stretching for twenty-five miles along both sides of the river, and stocked it with cattle; and announced plans to build a large slaughterhouse and packing plant to dress beef for shipment by refrigerator car to the eastern market. Until now, cattle raisers on the frontier had shipped their animals live to the Chicago stockyards. Morès believed that slaughtering the cattle near the range and shipping the dressed beef would be more efficient and would allow him to undersell the eastern meat packers. Icehouses at intervals along the railway line would protect the shipments against spoilage.

This was an impressive agenda for a twenty-five-year-old foreign aristocrat with no roots in the country and no experience in business. Yet at the end of six months he could claim success all along the line. An army of carpenters and masons was hard at work building Medora, with the packing plant as its centerpiece. His "chateau" was far enough along to permit him to bring his wife west in the autumn. In October he sent the first shipment of dressed beef rolling eastward in his new refrigerator cars; he had bought cattle for slaughtering from other ranchers in the region, as well as raising his own livestock. Word was spreading throughout western Dakota, eastern Montana, and even Wyoming that cattlemen no longer needed to deal with the Chicago beef barons; Morès was closer at hand, and paid better.

These brilliant successes, however, involved some serious risks. Morès's flamboyant life-style and his hard-driving tactics bred jealousy and suspicion among the ranchers of the region. Worse still, his decision to fence in his newly acquired range land ran counter to the accepted practice of sharing the open range. Nearby cattlemen found themselves cut off from access to the river; and squatters who had staked claims without benefit of legal papers found their hunting trails blocked by barbed wire and their claims challenged by the French interloper. Bad blood quickly built up to a crisis in June 1883. Three squatters, fortified by a visit to a Medora saloon, shot up the town, peppered Morès's half-finished chateau with their rifles, and gave him twenty-four hours to get out of town for good. Morès appealed to the sheriff, who sent a posse to arrest the troublemakers; but the sheriff's men were met and overawed by their quarry. Morès thereupon took things in his own hands: with two of his cowboys, he lay in wait for the three squatters as they rode toward their camp. In the firefight that followed, Morès killed one of the squatters, wounded another, and captured the third. The incident added to his reputation as a rough customer and crack shot, but it also brought serious complications. Arrested for murder, he was twice brought up for hearings before a justice of the peace, and was twice released on his plea of self-defense. But his enemies refused to let the matter die; two years later he was indicted by a grand jury, jailed for a month in Bismarck, and tried on the murder charge. Although acquitted, he emerged with a deep sense of grievance and a touch of paranoia about his persecutors. Sixteen times, he told a friend, he had been the target of rifle shots fired from ambush. The experience may have contributed to his eventual decision to leave Dakota—though business reverses were the principal reason.

For a time before his arrest and trial, however, his affairs had continued to prosper. By 1884, the "crazy Frenchman" had become a real celebrity. Newspapers from Bismarck to New York City carried feature stories about the "King of the Bad Lands"—the swash-buckling aristocrat dressed in colorful cowboy regalia, hunting big game with his wife riding and shooting alongside him. His "chateau" (actually an oversized ranch house) was the region's showplace; it boasted a staff of twenty servants, including a French chef, and champagne was the standard libation for visitors. Among those visitors was Theodore Roosevelt, who arrived in 1884 to take up cattle ranching nearby. Although Morès and Roosevelt had many traits in common, some doubted that Dakota was big enough to hold them both. Several disputes between them were resolved short of an open break; the most serious misunderstanding even threatened a duel which, if it had occurred, might easily have been fatal for the myopic Roosevelt.

Morès's fertile imagination continued to produce a stream of ideas for business ventures. He acquired another 12,000 acres of wheat land near Bismarck, to be leased out on a kind of sharecrop basis; he planted 50,000 cabbages as the beginning of a Little Missouri Valley truck farm; he inaugurated a stagecoach line to connect Medora with Deadwood in southern Dakota; he experimented with shipping Columbia River salmon from Oregon to New York City by refrigerator car. His packing plant by now was operating at capacity; his own land was stocked with 6,000 cattle, and he bought animals for slaughter from all comers, as distant as Wyoming. He took a flyer in sheep, bringing 15,000 head to his range, thus infuriating all cattlemen in the region. In short, Morès seemed to be on the way to becoming a tycoon of epic proportions—a frontier equivalent of the Fords, Rockefellers, and Armours.

All the more startling, therefore, was the rapid and complete disintegration of the Morès empire. One enterprise after another went sour. The sheep died during the hard winter of 1884–85. The stagecoach line went bankrupt in less than a year, when Morès failed to win a governmental mail contract. Worst of all, the centerpiece of his enterprises—the capture of the eastern market for beef—aroused the Chicago stockyard owners to emergency action. They banded together to close the market against this dangerous rival from the West, and drove him to the verge of bankruptcy. All this coincided with his arrest and trial in August–September 1885 on the old murder charge, from which he emerged triumphant but embittered. The Medora packing plant closed in the fall of 1886, and Morès departed for New York with his family. There he tried one last device to salvage something from the wreckage: he announced the creation of a consumers' meat cooperative designed to bypass the "beef trust" by delivering beef at reduced prices "direct from the rancher to the consumer." Shares in this venture were sold, and three meat supermarkets opened in New York City; but this venture too had to be liquidated after several months. Morès's Dakota career had cost him, according to various estimates, somewhere between a third of a million and a million and a half dollars (offset in part by the value of his Dakota real estate). His "chateau" in Medora remained in the family until 1936, when it was deeded to the North Dakota Historical Society. Caretakers had guarded the house and contents intact, down to the last china teacup. The town of Medora shriveled into near extinction until resurrected as a tourist attraction almost a century after its founding.

Morès was not a man to be downcast by failure. The urge for adventure and wealth remained as strong as ever; he was convinced that his enemies—notably what he called "the Jewish beef trust"—had brought him down, rather than any mistakes of his own. Back in Paris with his family for a time, they rejoined the social circuit and looked to the future. He was soon chafing for action, and late in 1887 set off for India and Nepal in the company of a prince of the Orleanist family to hunt tigers. Dakota had perfected his marksmanship; he bagged several tigers. But his association with the Orleanist pretender sparked rumors that they were plotting the restoration of the monarchy in France. Some of his enemies in Dakota had spread reports that Morès had boasted of even higher ambitions—using his fortune to win the throne for himself.

On the return voyage from India, Morès met some fellow Frenchmen on their way back from newly conquered Tonkin, in Indochina. Their talk of its rich possibilities kindled his imagination; he conceived the idea of building a railway from Hanoi to the remote interior, close to the Chinese border. In Paris he pestered government officials for support, promising to do the job without state subsidy; but he got no encouragement. He took off nevertheless for Hanoi, where he finally found a sympathetic listener in Governor-General Richaud. A quick trip into the interior convinced him that the scheme was feasible, and that the Chinese authorities would welcome a branch line into China itself. Back in Hanoi, he plunged into the task of recruiting engineers and laborers, and began construction. Again, frustration: orders came from Paris to stop work at once. Governor-General Richaud protested, blaming his predecessor in Hanoi, Ernest Constans, for the negative action in Paris; Richaud added that Constans had been neck deep in graft while in Indochina. Richaud was called home to report; but on the way, carrying what he said was incontrovertible evidence of Constans's misconduct, he was struck down by a lightning attack of cholera and buried with the evidence at sea. Morès meanwhile had been making his own way home to plead his case, but again he found no support. The railway project had to be abandoned, and the costs already incurred had to be borne by Morès himself. So ended, again in frustration, a second chapter in Morès's adventures.

Morès's arrival in Paris in March 1889 came at a moment of severe political crisis. For the past two years the Third Republic had been under sustained attack by General Georges Boulanger and his adherents, who had denounced the republic as flabby and corrupt, and had advocated an authoritarian system on Bonapartist lines. Parliamentary elections were due in September 1889, and the Boulangists seemed likely to win control. But shortly after Morès's return, a clever trick by Minister of Interior Ernest Constans led Boulanger to believe that he was about to be arrested and perhaps poisoned in prison; the General departed hastily for Brussels, and refused to return. In the absence of its figurehead, the Boulangist movement began to disintegrate; but Morès was drawn into its activities during those final months. His particular motive was to seek revenge against Constans, whom he blamed for his Indochina misadventure. Constans was up for reelection in Toulouse; Morès leaped into action in support of Constans's Boulangist rival. The campaign turned violent; Morès was arrested for pulling a revolver on a gang of Constans's backers who were threatening him. It was his first venture into politics, and it introduced the next important phase of his career.

In that phase, he emerged as a leading anti-Semitic agitator and, depending on definitions, as a protofascist. Morès was convinced by now that the Jews were at the root of all his personal failures. His suspicions were confirmed, he believed, when he read Edouard Drumont's *Jewish France*; published in 1886, it purported to prove that the Jews had infiltrated and corrupted every aspect of French life. Jewish capitalists, he already believed, had controlled the "beef trust" that had wrecked his American projects; a Jewish engineer in Indochina had betrayed him; a Jewish prefect in Toulouse had set him up for arrest during the election campaign. He joined the new French Antisemitic League when it was founded in 1889, and helped organize its first public meeting in early 1890, where he inflamed the crowd with an impassioned speech. When the League collapsed a few months later, he set up his own substitute called the Comité de la rue Sainte-Anne, later rebaptized "Morès et ses amis." He ran unsuccessfully for the Paris municipal council, announcing that "five years in North America made me a socialist" — but a "revisionist socialist," —quite different from the standard brand. In his speeches and brochures, Morès preached a strange mishmash of ideas: the right of property must be respected, "administrative tyranny" must be ended, freedom of association must be guaranteed to all, a system of "workers' credit" must be created, Jewish influence must be destroyed, the nation and the Church must be protected against their enemies. Some of his most fanatical supporters came from the stockyard district, where the butchers saw

Morès as their kind of leader. Morès recruited a private guard among them, providing uniforms in the form of sombreros and purple cowboy shirts: storm troopers before their time. His relations with the anarchists, who enjoyed a brief and sudden burst of notoriety in the early 1890s, were oddly ambiguous. He helped to finance an anarchist sheet, and once shared the platform with their firebrand activist Louise Michel, whom he embraced after she made an impassioned speech; but sometimes his meetings were disrupted by anarchists. If he deserved the label "friend of the workers," as he claimed, he was surely an odd sort of friend.

Indeed, Morès's activities won him more enemies than allies. He was challenged to duels by a series of prominent Jews, one of whom, Captain Meyer, he killed in a sword fight. He was arrested on this occasion, but acquitted at his trial. More painful to him was his father's repudiation of his demagogic appeals to the masses; consorting with anarchists was too much for the old duke. The government kept him under close scrutiny, and once jailed him for three months on the charge that he was plotting an outbreak of mass violence on May Day. Twice he was forced into embarrassing public admissions that he had accepted loans from prominent Jews in order to avert financial disaster. The Radical deputy Georges Clemenceau, who exposed one of these loans, paid a price for his temerity; Morès actively campaigned against him at the next elections and contributed to his defeat.

By the end of 1893, the anti-Semitic campaign was beginning to seem a bit stale. Even Drumont's virulent newspaper *Le Libre Parole*, to which Morès had contributed occasional articles, was losing readers. No one foresaw, of course, the coming resurgence of anti-Semitism that would accompany the Dreyfus affair. The passions aroused by that *cause célèbre* would have provided Morès with ideal conditions for his style of demagogy. For the moment, however, the racists were in retreat. Morès had lost none of his fanaticism, but he felt the urge to find another cause that would occupy his energies. That cause he found in Britain's imperialist rivalry with

France in Africa, and in Britain's alleged interference in French domestic affairs. The British, Morés believed, were not only seeking to block French expansion in Africa, but were also using Jewish Freemasons to manipulate such venal French politicians as Clemenceau. After helping to drive Clemenceau from Parliament on the allegation that he was a British agent, Morès turned to Africa as the logical place to strike another blow at perfidious Albion. He visited Algeria at the end of 1893, and stirred up crowds in several cities by speeches denouncing the British and the Jews. For the next two years he shuttled back and forth between Paris and Algeria, conferring with like-minded advisers and weighing several alternative schemes, none of them very precise. Sometimes he talked of crossing the desert to the upper Nile, with a view to forestalling Britain's efforts to move south from Cairo. Sometimes his destination was Lake Chad, where a population of 100 million (his calculation) was supposedly awaiting the benefits of French trade and culture. Sometimes he spoke in more exalted fashion: he would bring together the Latin Mediterranean countries—France, Spain, Italy—into an alliance with the Moslem world to challenge and roll back British influence in Africa.

By early 1896 he was ready to embark on this new adventure. He had already made a preliminary foray into southern Algeria, and had decided that a desert expedition was feasible; but he also concluded that the French authorities in Algeria were determined to block his plans because they feared trouble with the warlike desert tribe, the Tuaregs. He decided therefore to set off from southern Tunisia. Before leaving Paris on this final venture, a friend persuaded him to visit a palmist of some repute. She examined his hand but sat in gloomy silence until Morès urged her to speak. "You are about to depart on a great journey," she said reluctantly, "from which you will not return." Morès was shaken, but he concluded that his enemies in Paris were a greater danger than any menace the desert might hold. He spent a few weeks in Tunisia recruiting guides, interpreters, and camel-drivers, and set off on

May 14 in high spirits. The only European in the small band was Morès himself.

The expedition reached Tuareg country in early June, but its condition was precarious. Potable water had been almost impossible to find along the route; the camels were exhausted, the drivers and guides surly. At a remote oasis called El Ouatia Morès encountered a band of Tuaregs, and sought their help in recruiting guides and camels for the journey across the heart of the desert. After lengthy palavering, his Tunisian drivers were paid off and sent home, and he set off again, escorted by the Tuaregs. On June 9, these new escorts suddenly set upon Morès, dragged him from his mount, and struck him down with swords. Although seriously wounded, Morès fought back, killing three of his aggressors and holding the rest at bay for several hours. Then a couple of Tuaregs crept up from the rear and finished him off with guns and swords. Three days later, a Tunisian servant who escaped in the confusion brought the news to a French border post, whence the officer in charge sent a native detail to recover the body. The corpse reached Paris in July; Notre Dame Cathedral was packed for the funeral ceremony, and crowds followed the procession to Montmartre Cemetery. Some years later, the body was transferred to its final resting place in Cannes.

Morès's political ally Edouard Drumont, who spoke at the graveside service, along with Maurice Barrès, continued to insist that the Tuaregs were not the murderers; rather, he alleged, the Jews or perhaps the English had hired the assassins. Morès's widow haunted government offices for weeks in a futile effort to have the killers captured, but nothing was done. At one point she talked of bringing a band of Dakota cowboys, former employees of the marquis, to hunt down the assassins. At last she circulated a notice in North Africa offering a reward for the delivery of the culprits. This plan succeeded; in 1898 a desert chieftain tricked the three Tuareg killers into a rendezvous, seized them, and dropped them off at a French frontier post. They were not tried, however, until 1902, by which time one of the trio had died in prison. A second was sentenced to death (later commuted), and the third to twenty years at hard labor. Some years later an Italian admirer erected a large granite cross near the site of Morès's death. There were admirers in Paris too: at the height of the Dreyfus affair, Morès's friends commissioned a statue to be erected at the entrance to the Paris slaughterhouse "among the people he loved so well," but the city's municipal council refused permission. Eventually a statue was erected—but in Medora rather than Paris. Morès's children placed it there in 1926.

The marquis de Morès, someone has said, resembled a character out of Sue's *Mysteries of Paris*. It is true that he had some of those flamboyant, larger-than-life qualities that marked Sue's heroes. If he had returned safely from the Sahara at the height of the Dreyfus crisis (1898–1900), it is conceivable that man and moment might have coincided, and that he might have left a deeper mark on history. His charismatic personality, his demagogic talents, might have been the crystallizing force to rally the anti-Dreyfusards, the anti-Semites, and the right-wingers who had never been really reconciled to the republic. True, he might have been brought low by certain flaws of character, such as his impulsive nature, and his unwillingness to confront unpleasant facts. Still, it is fortunate that Morès was not available as the sword and voice of the anti-Dreyfusards in the moment of most intense crisis. France in the hands of Morès and his friends would have anticipated the fascist regimes of the twentieth century. It would be ironic if Frenchmen owed the survival of their liberal republic to a band of desert assassins.

M. LÉO TAXIL

7

Diana Vaughan
Satanist and Saint

In 1895, shortly before he departed on his fatal journey into the Sahara, the Marquis de Morès sent a gift to Miss Diana Vaughan—an Emmenthaler cheese, with a prayer carved into the rind. We can probably assume that there was no hidden symbolism in Morès's choice of a cheese to convey his admiration and respect, though who can be sure about human motives?. Diana was the current sensation of Paris, and was on the receiving end of a steady stream of fan mail and presents of all sorts. Her correspondents—all fervent Catholics—ranged across the spectrum from simple believers to parish priests and even bishops. The marquis, who professed an intense Catholic faith, was only one of many Frenchmen who saw Diana as a saintly figure, and a kind of reincarnation of Joan of Arc.

Diana was said to have been born of an American father and a French mother in Louisville, Kentucky, in 1874. Vaughan *père* ranked high in the Palladian order, the highest and most secret inner circle of Freemasonry. Among Diana's distant ancestors was the seventeenth-century English Rosicrucian Thomas Vaughan, who in 1645 had married the goddess Astarte. The Palladian order, headed in the United States by General Albert Pike, was dedicated to the worship of Lucifer in his timeless struggle to destroy Christianity. Diana, at the tender age of five, was chosen by General Pike to become the high priestess of the Palladians, and was put through a rigorous training course to prepare her for this vocation. She was affianced to the god Asmodeus and accompanied him on quick visits to the nether regions and to various planets. But when the great day came for the final ceremony that would induct her into the office of high priestess, she unaccountably rebelled against those who had selected and trained her: she refused to spit upon the Holy Eucharist. Her outraged sponsors moved to replace her with one Sophie Walder, daughter of a devil, though with a more earthly Mormon connection as well. Diana, however, refused to give up her claim to be high priestess, and organized a schismatic branch of the Luciferian order. From her new headquarters in Paris, she began to publish a monthly journal attacking both her rival Sophie and the Catholic Church.

Then came salvation. In June 1895 Joan of Arc appeared to Diana and converted her to the true faith; she fled to a convent outside Paris and remained in seclusion while repenting of her sins. But she promptly began to publish tracts exposing the secrets of her past life and of Freemasonry, beginning with her own confessions entitled *Memoirs of an Ex-Palladian*. A steady flow of publications followed: a book of hymns, a prayer book, volumes of poetry, anti-Masonic brochures, a monthly journal. Diana's conversion and her revelation of Freemasonry's activity in the service of Satan created a sensation. Her business agent, the journalist Léo Taxil (himself a convert to Catholicism after years of anticlerical activity), promoted Diana's writings with energy and skill. Many Catholic newspapers took up her cause against the skeptics and critics; parish priests urged their flocks to read her revelations of Masonic machinations; several bishops endorsed her campaign, and the Pope himself was moved to give his blessing to her book of prayers. Taxil helped Diana in her crusade by organizing an Anti-Masonic Union with chapters in many French cities. The movement transcended frontiers: an Anti-Masonic Congress was convened in Italy in September 1896. Taxil attended, and sought to defend Diana against the challenges of doubters.

As Diana's crusade gained momentum, the voices of the skeptics and critics grew louder. Freemasons and freethinkers were of course outraged by her revelations, but many faithful Catholics also viewed Diana's campaign with rising concern. They suspected a hoax and feared its damaging effects on the Church; some of them suggested that Diana did not exist, but was merely an invention of Taxil. At one point Taxil sought to confound the doubters by staging a press conference at which he presented both Diana and a Dr. Bataille, another author of anti-Masonic works which Taxil had published. But only a few true believers were admitted to this affair, and they were easily satisfied. The wave of protest kept growing and intensified when "Dr. Bataille" publicly confessed that he had participated with Taxil in an elaborate hoax. Taxil countered by charging that the Freemasons had bribed the doctor to make a false confession, but his explanations were no longer enough. He announced, therefore, that Diana would appear before the general public in April 1897 and would respond in person to the skeptics.

On the appointed evening the rented auditorium (down the boulevard a short distance from Saint-Germain-des-Prés) was packed to the rafters with a mixed crowd of true believers and critics. Taxil shrewdly built up the tension, explaining that Diana would arrive at any moment, and raffling off a typewriter to pass the time. The denouement came at last: Taxil launched into a two-hour harangue detailing how for twelve years he had carried on what he called "the greatest hoax in modern history." Diana, he confessed, did not exist outside his imagination; neither did the Palladian order. His own conversion to Catholicism had been faked; the purpose of his hoax was to reveal the ignorance and bigotry of the Church establishment; he remained what he had always been, a Freemason and freethinker. While his audience sat stunned, Taxil hastily departed under the protection of a handful of friends and ten policemen. In the words of a journalist present in the auditorium, Taxil's revelations were greeted by "an indescribable tumult." The furious crowd pursued Taxil to a nearby café where he had taken refuge, shouting "A l'eau" ("To the river!"), but the police detail warded them off. Despite this shocking exposé, some churchmen, including one bishop, clung stubbornly to their belief that Diana was real. They charged that Taxil and the Freemasons had put her out of the way by confinement or murder.

Diana Vaughan's true identity (or nonidentity) having been established, there remains the question of Léo Taxil: who was he, and how was he able to perpetrate such a gigantic hoax? Taxil was born Gabriel Jogand-Pagès in Marseille in 1854, the son of a well-to-do Catholic and royalist businessman. He was educated in Catholic schools and earned an early reputation as a practical joker and troublemaker. Expelled from his *lycée* for leading a student protest, he attached himself to the republican opposition in Marseille and wrote newspaper articles attacking Napoleon III. When the Second Empire was overthrown in 1870, he broke with his family, adopted the pseudonym Léo Taxil, and was briefly involved in the Marseille Commune of 1871. For several years thereafter he published a violently anticlerical newspaper in Marseille; he consorted with a low-life crowd, and was repeatedly accused and convicted of libel. By 1876 he had accumulated so many unpaid fines that he found it convenient to depart into Swiss exile.

Two years sufficed to make him persona non grata in Geneva as well. On the verge of expulsion by the Swiss authorities, a general amnesty in France allowed him to return, and he decided to try his luck in Paris. He opened an anticlerical bookshop and publishing house in the Latin Quarter, and found his real vocation at last, as author of scurrilously anti-Catholic pamphlets. The titles alone were enough to infuriate good churchgoers: among them were *The Pope's Mistresses*, *The Jesuit's Son*, *The Secret Books of the Confessors*, and *Down With the Priests*! The content of these tracts was as offensive as the titles: Taxil shamelessly invented stories of priestly misconduct, and introduced enough pornography to extend the market. The sales figures were heartening: most of the brochures sold from twenty to forty thousand copies, while one reached a peak of 130,000. Taxil turned out six or eight of these items each year for the next six years, which brought him a tidy income, though part of it went into paying fines for defamation. Ingenious as always, he founded a French Anticlerical League with branches in many cities, and even some in Spain. This network served admirably to market his works. He was encouraged for a time to think of a political career: he ran for the Paris municipal council in 1880, and for the Chamber of Deputies in 1881, but without success. In Paris, campaigning against the noted anti-Semite Edouard Drumont, he polled a total of three votes.

Suddenly in 1885 Parisians were startled to learn that this scourge of the Church had himself gotten religion. He informed the world that in the course of reading the records of Joan of Arc's trial, he had miraculously recovered his faith. Some skeptics put forward a more cynical explanation: sales of Taxil's brochures had been falling off lately, suggesting that his message had gone stale. Such was indeed the case; but in addition he was harassed by repeated lawsuits, and was beginning to suffer from sheer boredom as well. He had used up all of the antichurch scurrilities that his imagination could produce.

Taxil's "conversion" gave him a new lease on life. With fresh energy, he set out to expose the sins and misdeeds of his former associates, the Freemasons. Books, brochures, a magazine, and a newspaper carried his revised message: the Freemasons, operating clandestinely, had gained control of the republic's levers of power, and were busily undermining all of the solid institutions of France. The Church, which was gravely threatened by this merciless adversary, was the principal bulwark against the destroyers; it alone could save the nation. Taxil's born-again works sold as well as their predecessors, though of course to a quite different audience. Catholic press organs hailed his conversion, and published enthusiastic reviews as each of his brochures appeared. The papal nuncio called him in for a talk, and lifted the several excommunications he had collected in prior years. He was invited to Rome in 1887, and was given a private audience with Pope Leo XIII, who pointed proudly to a collection of Taxil's writings (the recent ones) on the shelf of his study. Seventeen bishops contributed favorable blurbs to be used in the preface of one of his books.

Eight years of this intense pro-clerical activity left Taxil rather jaded; he needed novelty and a new angle. He found it when in 1893 he met Dr. Charles Hacks, a boyhood friend from Marseille who had traveled throughout the world as a ship's physician. Taxil persuaded Hacks to provide local color for a book which Taxil would write under the pseudonym of Dr. Bataille. This two-volume work, entitled *The Devil in the Nineteenth Century*, purported to recount the curious experiences of Dr. Bataille (Hacks) in exotic corners of the world. The focus, even more than earlier, was on the nefarious schemes of the Freemasons and other "Satanic" secret societies. It was Dr. Bataille who claimed to have discovered the ultrasecret Palladian cult, headquartered in Charleston, South Carolina, and headed by the "anti-Pope" Albert Pike. The Palladians, he reported, aimed to displace the true Pope in favor of their own anti-Pope. Their membership extended to both sexes, and their rituals naturally included orgies of the most disgusting sort. Lutherans, the doctor revealed, were in fact worshippers of Lucifer; England was already in the grip of disciples of Satan. Dr. Bataille reported that Satan had installed workshops in caves beneath Gibraltar, where infamous black-Mass objects were produced along with cultures of disease germs destined to spread plagues throughout the Catholic world. To reduce disbelief, Dr. Bataille provided quantified evidence: the number of infernal spirits in the underworld, he declared, was 44,435,633. He also detailed a bizarre story of an acquaintance who had been invited to a séance at the home of a London aristocrat. "It was a Saturday, the day consecrated to Moloch. Suddenly the table that had just revolved on command leaped to the ceiling, then fell again to the floor, and then suddenly was transformed into a horrible winged crocodile. But surprise reached its climax when the crocodile was seen to approach the piano, open it and play a melody of the weirdest sort. And while he played, the winged crocodile looked toward the mistress of the house and ogled her lasciviously." Someone has suggested that this may have been the earliest manifestation of punk rock.

Dr. Bataille's book was an immediate success. Issued by a reputable Catholic publishing house, it was advertised throughout the French Catholic world, and was warmly recommended by many clerics. Dr. Hacks did well enough from his share of the proceeds to abandon his medical career and buy a restaurant. As for Taxil, he was encouraged to dip still deeper into his imagination. Among the discoveries of Dr. Bataille in the United States had been the beautiful young Palladian Diana Vaughan. In 1895 Taxil made her the centerpiece of his new enterprise, recounting in *Memoirs of an Ex-Palladian* her life as a Satanist and her conversion to the true faith. That story has already been told; there remains only to explain, insofar as possible, how Taxil was able to pull off so elaborate a hoax.

The easiest explanation, no doubt, would be to resort to P. T. Barnum's classic dictum that a sucker is born every minute. That, however, can hardly provide the whole answer in a nation like France whose citizens have always prided themselves on their sophistication and skepticism. Some special factors must have been at work there toward the end of the nineteenth century—factors that allowed thousands of supposedly educated and enlightened citizens to swallow the outrageous inventions of a hack journalist. Something in the mental climate of the time must have weakened resistance to the contagion.

The central factor surely must have been the cumulative effect of the religious war that had divided Frenchmen for the past half-century. Conflicts over the Catholic church's role in society and the state had persisted ever since the Revolution of 1789, and had grown more intense since the mid-nineteenth century. A kind of counter-church had emerged as positivist doctrine spread, with its emphasis on science and reason, and its institutional manifestation in Freemasonry. These secular humanists were seen by Catholics as a grave threat to the true faith; and they in turn viewed the Church as the embodiment of a bigoted conservatism as well as the sworn enemy of republicanism. Although moderates on both sides favored a live-and-let-live philosophy, extremist voices tended to drown out the compromisers and to inflame passions in a kind of bloodless holy war. Each side mistrusted the other and branded the enemy as subversive.

A second factor contributed to the tension. The priesthood in nineteenth-century France, except for a highly intellectual élite, was recruited for the most part from country boys with little or no education beyond the local seminary near their homes. Their limited and narrow training, their restricted opportunity to see anything of the world beyond their backwoods parish, scarcely fitted them for understanding the nature of the modern world. Faith was exalted as higher than reason; truth was confined to the Church's official pronouncements. Parish priests looked to the Catholic press, to the bishops, and of course to the Pope for guidance on any matter of controversy. And from none of these in the late nineteenth century did they get much enlightenment. They were told constantly that the anticlericals and the Freemasons were deadly enemies out to destroy the Church. Papal encyclicals repeatedly affirmed this belief: Pius IX in 1873 declared Freemasonry to be the work of Satan, and Leo XIII in 1884 proclaimed that the human race was divided between those who served Christ and those who served Satan. All Freemasons, he added, belonged to the second category; bishops were enjoined to expose their maleficent purposes and actions. With the highest church authority reinforcing their instinctive beliefs (and with some noisy anticlerical extremists feeding the fears of gullible believers), it is not surprising that so many Catholic laymen and priests were taken in by Taxil's gross inventions. Looking back from our own time, one leading Catholic historian has remarked with embarrassment: "We must admit that in this period French Catholics demonstrated a truly exceptional naiveté." It should be added, however, that many Catholics and many anticlericals never did swallow Taxil's fabulations in either their first or their second phase. Some of these skeptics were amused, others irritated; but they chose to stand aloof from what they saw as a ridiculous squabble between factions of irrational fanatics.

Still a third factor may have contributed, at least marginally, to Taxil's success as a *mystificateur*. The last two decades of the century brought a mild resurgence of interest in things supernatural. Spiritualist séances, which had enjoyed such a vogue in the 1850s, had retained some adepts ever since, but they took on new life in the 1890s. Occultism in various forms found adherents, perhaps as a backlash against the arid rigors of positivism. Novels like those of J.K. Huysmans reflected this mood. This phenomenon, along with the Church hierarchy's insistence that Satan and his agents were real and omnipresent, made it easier for Taxil to get a hearing for his fantasies about gods, devils, and winged crocodiles.

Taxil, like his creature Diana Vaughan, disappeared from the spotlight after the famous meeting where his hoax was disclosed. He republished some of his anticlerical brochures, wrote a few pornographic novels, and produced one final antimasonic tract in which a pseudonymous priest accused Taxil of having sequestered or murdered Diana. These ventures attracted little notice, and Taxil retreated into more innocuous activities such as publishing cookbooks. He died in 1907 in almost total obscurity, respected by his neighbors in suburban Sceaux as a solid bourgeois family man who kept to himself, as a proper neighbor should.

Guth del.

Revue Illustrée.

Florian sc.

M. CONSTANS
Ministre de l'Intérieur.

8

Ernest Constans
Political Buccaneer

The British scholar Lord Bryce, visiting the United States toward the end of the nineteenth century, found that among Americans "politician is a term of reproach." Bryce might have reached the same conclusion had he visited France in that era. There, too, politicians in the newly established Third Republic were not highly esteemed, even though the game of politics quickly became one of France's leading spectator sports. As in modern professional football, rival teams of gladiators performed in the arena while their passionately partisan adherents followed the action from the sidelines; most citizens meanwhile paid only sporadic and distracted attention to these elaborate games. The professionals who made up the so-called political class enjoyed a mixed reputation among committed and indifferent spectators alike. The most successful ones were admired for their skills and courted for their ability to distribute favors; but they were not often praised for their sterling character. Perhaps that was because politics tends to attract clever manipulators rather than paragons of virtue. Or perhaps the French, like the Americans, were inclined to judge their elected representatives with more cynicism than charity, hoping for the best but expecting the opposite. Yet even though most Frenchmen were mordant critics of their political class, they were probably more tolerant than Americans in condoning their moral lapses. After all, as Frenchmen saw it, politicians too are human.

Ernest Constans would seem to be a case in point. For thirty years he sat in Parliament, only once failing of reelection. He served in four cabinets in the key post of minister of interior; on several occasions he was talked of as a possible premier, and twice he was a serious candidate for the presidency of the Senate. In a moment of severe crisis for the regime, he was credited with saving the republic from the threat of a potential dictator. Repeatedly frustrated in his ambition to head the government, he turned late in life from politics to diplomacy; he became France's ambassador to Turkey in 1898, and remained in that delicate post for nine years. Yet despite this impressive record, the taint of scandal clung to him throughout his public career. Many of his contemporaries suspected him, or openly accused him, of shameless venality, of unscrupulous resort to brutal police methods, of opportunism and avidity for power; and historians, when they have mentioned him at all, have been inclined to perpetuate that image. What moderns might call "the sleaze factor" did in the end blight his highest ambitions, yet it never drove him out of public life; the voters in Toulouse remained faithful, and his party colleagues rose to his defense against partisan attacks. Perhaps his career suggests that the French are, or were then, unduly relaxed about rascals in politics. Or perhaps he was actually better than he seemed; if he refused to answer the character assassins who hounded him, this may have been evidence of his profound contempt for them rather than a silent admission of guilt.

Constans was a man of the Midi, born in Béziers in 1833, nurtured and educated in Toulouse. Southerners in France are supposed to be nonstop talkers and genial backslappers. If so, Constans was atypical; he was always sparing with words and, as someone has put it, "concealed beneath his southern joviality a phlegmatic Dutch temperament." Politics for him was a matter of cutting deals in the corridors rather than engaging in oratorical jousts in the Chamber. Constans's origins were bourgeois; his father was a moderately prosperous mortgage officer who left him a small inheritance. He studied law in Toulouse, was appointed at age twenty-two to the public prosecutor's staff in his home city, and married the daughter of a small town businessman-entrepreneur from the region. But within a year of this promising start his fortunes turned sour; he was dismissed from his judicial post and apparently wasted his inheritance in gambling and high living. He left for Barcelona to seek his fortune and tried several business experiments there, one of which was later to excite the interest of his political enemies. With a Spanish partner he set up business as a *vidangeur*, manufacturing and operating mobile pumps used to empty cesspools. To his critics, it seemed to foreshadow his later political career; they never missed a chance to call him *le vidangeur*. The enterprise failed, in any case, and Constans returned to Toulouse not only penniless but in debt. For many years a cloak of mystery hung over his early years in Toulouse and Barcelona, inspiring noxious rumors. Eventually, at the peak of his career, the rumors were to develop into a damaging exposé.

On his return from Spain, Constans resumed his legal studies. After a year of independent cramming for the *agrégation*, he succeeded in the examination in 1871, and thus qualified for a university teaching post. He spent a few years on various law faculties, but politics for him had greater attraction than pedagogy; he won election to the Toulouse municipal council and then to the post of vice-mayor. When the Third Republic was formally established in 1875, he raised his sights to a seat in Parliament; in 1876, at the age of forty-two, he was elected to the Chamber of Deputies. There he joined the moderate republican party led by the charismatic Léon Gambetta and informally called the Opportunists.

His rise was strikingly rapid. Within four years he was named to a subcabinet post, and six months later was promoted to the powerful position of minister of interior and religious affairs. He held that post for the next eighteen months, under two successive premiers; and in the process he earned a reputation as a tough and efficient administrator. As interior minister, he was charged with maintaining public order through his control of the police, and with supervising local government and national elections through his provincial agents, the prefects. As minister of religious affairs (Cults), he was called upon to begin the process of separating church and state, in conformity with the republicans' anticlerical principles.

Constans plunged into all these tasks with ruthless energy. His methods were brutally explicit. It was said that he dealt with his prefects with a jovial smile and an iron fist: "You will kindly do thus and so, Mr. Prefect." "But Mr. Minister, that's impossible." "I don't ask you whether it is possible. I tell you to do it. We understand each other, don't we, my dear prefect? That's all I have to say. Good day, my dear prefect." The method worked. The first step in the new anticlerical policy was the expulsion of certain religious orders, notably the Jesuits, those longtime *bêtes noires* of the republicans. Constans ignored the violent protests of the political right and the church; the expulsions were carried out with no disturbance of public order. Meanwhile he also mobilized his police against the Radical republicans headed by Georges Clemenceau, who wanted to stage a public demonstration celebrating the tenth anniversary of the Paris Commune. The police broke up the demonstration, infuriating the radicals but impressing his moderate allies with his toughness. But the real proof of his skills came during the legislative elections of 1881. Constans made clear to his prefects that he expected them to produce a republican majority, and that they should use whatever pressures and inducements might be needed. The outcome was a smashing success; the opportunists' grip on power was solidly established.

When Jules Ferry's cabinet fell late in 1881, there was serious talk of Constans as his successor. But his more squeamish political allies were concerned about his severe police methods, and about rumors that he had enriched himself while minister, presumably by tapping a secret fund available to him for convenient subsidies. He reverted therefore to his role as simple deputy, although each cabinet crisis thereafter brought new talk of him as potential premier. Instead, the government in 1886 sent him on a special diplomatic mission to China to negotiate a trade treaty, and a year later named him the first governor-general of French Indo-China. But his high-handed independence in that post offended his bureaucratic superior in Paris: he was summoned home to explain his actions, and resigned after a wrangle with his chief. His conduct as governor-general continued to haunt him, however; his successor in Hanoi, a career colonial administrator named Richaud, sent off a series of reports accusing Constans of grievous misdeeds, ranging from policy blunders to accepting bribes from Chinese gambling-house operators. Constans, he alleged, had even taken a payoff from the king of Cambodia in the form of a priceless gold belt studded with diamonds. An inquiry was opened, and Richaud was ordered home with the damning evidence. But by the time he sailed, the wheel of fortune had turned again in Constans's favor; in 1889 he was named to his old post as minister of interior, with the police at his disposal. When Richaud's ship reached Ceylon, it was reported that the governor-general had died en route from a sudden attack of cholera, and had been buried at sea with all his baggage. An uproar followed; some right-wing politicians challenged Constans on the floor of Parliament, relating the rumors of Richaud's charges that had been circulating. Constans sat through their accusations, then struck back vigorously. He had asked or received no bribes, he said; the jeweled belt was the king's own sword belt offered as a simple token of friendship; the jewels in it were false. The Chamber overwhelmingly approved his defense, and the matter died. But the suspicion of skulduggery in Hanoi continued to cloud Constans's reputation from that time forward. As for the suspicion that he had arranged to have Richaud poisoned while en route home, he scoffed privately, "I do my own assassinating."

Meanwhile Constans was about to enter on his finest hour. During his absence in Hanoi, a serious threat to the republic had blown up in the person of General Georges Boulanger, a charismatic army officer who aspired to a political role. Boulanger's initial sponsors were radical republicans like Clemenceau who hoped that the general would rid France of the flabby opportunist lawyer-politicians and would install a strong presidential regime with an aggressive foreign policy. Through 1887 and 1888, Boulanger's name was entered in a series of by-elections to the Chamber, and in most cases he won. This piecemeal plebiscite was plainly designed to culminate in the general elections of 1889, when Boulanger proposed to head a ticket in every district and thus to be swept into power with a mandate to revise the constitution. A final by-election in January 1889, this time in the republicans' stronghold of Paris itself, gave Boulanger his most stunning victory. The survival of the parliamentary republic was now in serious question. Indeed, things were even worse than either the opportunist or the radical republicans realized; privately, Boulanger was in touch with both the monarchist and the Bonapartist pretenders and was receiving subsidies from them. The republican leaders, desperate for a way to block the Boulangist juggernaut, turned to Constans. They remembered his expert management of the 1881 elections, and hoped that he might work a second miracle. A cabinet reshuffle in February 1889 restored him to the interior ministry. His ruthless methods, they thought, might work again.

Constans's real intentions at this critical point were not fully clear, nor do historians agree even now. Some of them believe that Constans took office with all his options open—including the possibility of climbing aboard Boulanger's victory car. It is true that on his return from Indo-China a few months earlier, he had accepted an invitation to dine with the general and to talk confidentially about the political scene. The dinner had been cancelled when Boulanger fell briefly ill, and Constans soon developed some doubts about the general's strength of character. Even so, when he was restored to the interior ministry with the police and the prefects at his disposal, Constans may have been tempted by the prospect of becoming Boulanger's strong man. If so, he was quickly disillusioned; the Boulangists chose to attack him rather than to win him over. They seized on a court case that allegedly involved Constans in a payoff from a shady insurance company that had used his name in its brochures. Boulangist spokesmen brought the matter to the floor of Parliament, but Constans struck back energetically. The company, he asserted, had used his name without his permission; he had received an honorarium, but had not cashed the check and had eventually returned it. True, he admitted, he had received gifts from the company: an Arab rifle and a Lyonnais sausage. "I returned the gun; as for the sausage, I ate it." The Chamber greeted his defense with an ovation, and rejected the Boulangist challenge. If Constans until now had been weighing his options, he was no longer in any doubt; he would deal with Boulanger in his own way.

His way was not to risk confronting Boulanger at the polls (a risky prospect), but to use a calculated combination of threat and bluff. If he could expose Boulanger as a seriously flawed hero, the general's bubble of popularity might burst. Constans set out, therefore, to set and bait his trap. He persuaded Parliament to organize the Senate as a high court, and he spread the rumor that Boulanger and his top aides would be arrested and tried by that court on charges of subversion. Hints were also dropped that poison might turn up in the prison food. What happened next has been related in several versions, but the essential fact is that Constans's scheme worked. At the crucial moment in his disinformation campaign, he invited one of Boulanger's friends to come to the ministry, and arranged to be called out of the office briefly on the expectation that the visitor would glance over the papers on his desk. Prominently exposed was a note ordering Boulanger's arrest. When the minister returned, the visitor was on his way to warn the general, who caught the next train to Brussels. At the frontier, Constans's police agents telegraphed the news, and the minister staged an impromptu champagne celebration. The Boulangist wave was broken; the general's adherents fell to squabbling and exposing inside secrets. The republic was saved.

Constans's triumph left him solidly esconced as the dominant figure in the cabinet, where he continued his reign for an almost unprecedented three years. But he was to pay a heavy price for his victory, for the angry Boulangists were burning to exact vengeance. They tried first to defeat him at the polls; in the 1889 elections they brought toughs and agitators, including the Marquis de Morès, to Toulouse to harass his backers and break up his election rallies. They should have known that Constans was experienced in such tactics; his police and prefect struck back ruthlessly. Next they turned to a more effective strategy, calling on the talents of the poison-pen pamphleteer Henri Rochefort, who had been exiled to England along with several other leading Boulangists. Rochefort, who could certainly compete with Constans in unscrupulousness, set out to destroy the minister by exposing the seamy side of his past. He sent a henchman to Toulouse to dig up evidence of Constans's youthful transgressions, and the agent brought back a bonanza which Rochefort then elaborated into a series of scurrilous articles in his Paris daily *L'Intransigeant*. After hinting, without visible evidence, that Constans as a teenager had been expelled from *lycée* for cheating, and alleging that the minister's father-in-law had served time in prison for fraudulent bankruptcy, Rochefort charged that Constans had misspent part of his youth as a croupier, and that he still owned a gambling den in Toulouse called the Café Divan. After these mild preliminaries, Rochefort turned serious: at age twenty-two, he asserted, Constans had been involved in a flagrant case of child abuse. Through a procurer, he was said to have bought a thirteen-year-old girl from the latter's mother, and was accused of "violences" on the child's person. At the subsequent trial where mother and procurer were given jail terms, Constans had appeared only as a witness, but he had received a tongue-lashing from the judge, who declared that he ought to be in the dock along with the offenders. Constans's connections in town had apparently enabled him to escape that disgrace, but he was immediately dismissed from his post in the prosecutor's office and found it expedient after a time to depart into Spanish exile. There, too, Rochefort pursued him with allegations; the banker Puig y Puig had made him a sizable business loan which Constans had been unable to repay; the banker had died shortly afterward in mysterious circumstances. In full cry now, Rochefort continued to pile up charges. He resurrected the accusations of bribery and financial malversation from Indo-China days, and openly accused Constans of arranging the assassination of Richaud to suppress the latter's testimony.

Rochefort's maledictions lost some of their impact through his reputation for vituperative scandal-mongering and unreliability. Even so, the charges were explicit enough to suggest that they were not mere inventions. Constans's colleagues in the cabinet were distressed, and urged him to present counter-evidence or to sue Rochefort for slander, but he stubbornly refused to respond. Rochefort set out therefore to administer the *coup de grace*; he called on his Boulangist allies in Parliament to interpellate Constans by reading out the *Intransigeant* articles in public session. On January 19, 1892 Deputy Francis Laur attempted to do so, only to be promptly silenced by the presiding officer. But Laur had managed to convey his purpose and to get in a few verbal slashes—enough to provoke Constans at last into furious action. As Laur descended from the rostrum, Constans sprang up from his bench and delivered a pair of resounding slaps to his accuser's face. Laur retaliated by flinging a copy of the *Manual of Parliamentary Law* at Constans's head, but missed his target and hit another minister instead. According to the Chamber's stenographic record, *"agitation prolongée"* followed; most deputies left their seats and engaged in a free-for-all until the presiding officer managed to suspend the session. When the Chamber reconvened, Constans had recovered his usual aplomb. He apologized to the house, reminding his colleagues that in seventeen years he had never been censured for parliamentary misconduct. He was given a standing ovation; for the next half-hour friendly deputies filed past to shake his hand and assure him of their sympathy. Laur, after some procrastination, sent his seconds to challenge Constans, but the minister refused to fight. The crisis passed; it seemed that Constans had ridden it out. But appearances were misleading; some of the mud thrown by Rochefort stuck to him. His colleagues in the cabinet found his presence embarrassing, and soon arranged to replace him as minister. Never again was he to serve in a cabinet. His resentment was deep, but he managed to put up a brave front.

As he lost power in 1892, the republic was about to be faced by another severe trauma—the affair known as the Panama scandal. Some years earlier, when the Panama Company was struggling to complete the canal across the isthmus, company officials desperate to raise capital had bribed a considerable number of deputies and journalists to authorize and recommend a lottery loan. When the company failed, rumors of payoffs began to spread, and angry shareholders demanded an investigation. A few names began to leak out, and the republican leaders were reluctantly driven to set up a commission of inquiry. It may seem surprising, given Constans's reputation for venality, that his name never appeared on any payoff list. Perhaps this suggests that he was less venal than painted. But there is another possible explanation; he was far away in Indo-China during the period when most of the bribing went on. His only Panama involvement was marginal. Shortly before he was dropped from the cabinet, a Panama official showed him a partial list of politicians who had accepted bribes. Constans had the list photographed before returning it, and instead of keeping or destroying it, handed it over to his successor. He was suspected also of giving a copy to the editor of a Boulangist newspaper, *La Cocarde*, who proceeded to publish the names. His presumed motive was to embarrass his Opportunist colleagues for having excluded him from the cabinet.

Some years earlier, Constans had exchanged his seat in the Chamber of Deputies for one in the more quiescent Senate. He remained active there, sponsoring such social reform legislation as a public welfare system in rural areas and a pension fund for workers. In 1896 he declared his candidacy for the presidency of the Senate; and though he lost, he polled a respectable vote. Constans and his wife engaged little in the social whirl of Paris; apparently they lacked both interest and any social graces. Edmond de Goncourt, who encountered them at a dinner party, recorded his distaste in his journal: "An ugly couple, the Constans menage! The husband with the look of a gendarme in mufti, a heavy jaw, and the unpleasant thick accent of the Midi. The wife, with the clear eye of a jaybird under wrinkled eyelids, a muddled complexion, an ill-designed mouth that emits curt replies to the remarks of other guests." As usual, Goncourt dipped his pen in vitriol.

When Constans's first term in the Senate ended in 1897, he anticipated easy reelection. He was wrong: his enemies recruited a strong rival candidate who triumphed by a single vote. Constans's supporters prepared to contest the result when the new Senate met; but shortly before Parliament convened, the victorious rival dropped dead, and the Senate promptly validated Constans as the runner-up. Critics were struck by the way chance repeatedly intervened to clear Constans's path of rivals and enemies: at crucial moments, sudden death had removed Governor-General Richaud of Indo-China, the Spanish banker Puig y Puig, and now the only competitor who had beaten him at the polls. Hostile journalists suspected that something more than mere coincidence must be involved; some of them referred to him as "Constans-Borgia." Earlier they had labeled him "Fouché-Constans," linking him with the memory of the first Napoleon's feared chief of police. Constans, as usual, brushed off the epithets, with one exception that he rather liked: *le vieux forban*," which translates as "the old buccaneer."

In 1898, to almost everyone's surprise, Constans was appointed ambassador to Turkey, a post normally held by a diplomatic professional. The announcement raised some eyebrows, for he had no special expertise in Near Eastern affairs, and his earlier diplomatic ventures in China and Indo-China had hardly been shining successes. Why did Constans accept a post that would remove him from his natural milieu of parliamentary politics? Quite clearly, because he calculated it as a chance for political gain. Privately, he told an acquaintance (who happened to be a police informer as well) that he intended to stay in Constantinople for only three or four months, until the uproar over the Dreyfus affair had died down.

He was, said Constans, on good terms with both sides in the Drey-fus dispute; a convenient absence at the height of the conflict would strengthen his chances of regaining a ministerial post, perhaps even the premiership. As usual, Constans kept all options open, and cultivated allies on both or all sides. To protect his political base, he arranged to retain his Senate seat while serving as ambassador. Only two months after arriving in Turkey, the presidency of the Senate fell vacant, and Constans hastened home to try again for that post. As before, however, he was outvoted, even though he won substantial support. He turned therefore with greater serious-ness to his ambassadorial duties, though for a couple of years there were recurrent rumors in Paris that he would soon be called back as premier or as minister of foreign affairs. Neither he nor anyone else imagined that he would remain in Constantinople for almost a decade.

Constans's term as ambassador was marked by intense great-power rivalries in Turkey over trade, investment, and railway-build-ing. His dispatches to the Quai d'Orsay suggest that he was an active emissary, determined to speak out in defense of French pres-tige in the region and to advance the ambitions of French traders and investors. He believed in France's destiny as an imperial power, with national interest and private profit as the proper drives for imperial expansion. He also believed in cozying up to the Turkish authorities, and especially to Sultan Abdul Hamid, who quickly identified the ambassador as a kindred spirit. The flagrant corrup-tion of the Sultan's court—and of the Sultan himself—obviously did not offend this cynical Frenchman; Abdul Hamid openly ad-mired Constans's toughness and lack of scruple, and went out of his way to show his favor. Indeed, reports reached Paris that at one point the Sultan half-jokingly proposed to make Constans his grand vizier, suggesting that he would willingly pay him ten times his ambassadorial salary. Paris journalists alleged that Constans had found his post a lucrative base for lining his own pockets; there were rumors of a million-franc payoff for arranging a contract with a French firm to build naval vessels for Turkey, and two million for expediting a mining concession for a French company. British embassy officials, who disliked and distrusted him, privately called him "Monsieur 12 per cent"; the French Socialist daily *Humanité* inflated that figure, alleging that everyone in Turkey knew Constans as "Monsieur 18 per cent." When revolution came to Turkey in 1908, Constans claimed that he sympathized with the reform goals of the Young Turks; but the new leaders wanted nothing to do with a crony of the deposed Sultan. Isolated, Constans gave up his post in 1909.

Despite his advanced age of seventy-six, Constans could not face the idea of retirement. He had given up his Senate seat some years earlier, but he hoped for a comeback in the 1910 elections. That effort failed; reluctantly, he slipped out of public life and public notice. His wife had died in 1906, in part from complications resulting from an attack by an enraged ram in the gardens of the ambassador's summer residence. When Constans in turn died in 1913, shortly after his eightieth birthday, the obituaries were surprisingly generous. *L'Illustration* praised him as "one of the most subtle and far-sighted political figures of our time"; the semi-official daily *Le Temps* devoted a full front-page column to his career. Although he was a lifetime anticlerical, it was reported that a priest attended him in his last moments. But his funeral ceremony was hardly orthodox; it took place in the waiting-room of the Gare d'Austerlitz, whence his body was to be shipped to his country home (often described as a chateau) in the Aveyron department. A considerable crowd of politicians and government officials attended; the only speaker was Minister of Interior Klotz, who exalted Constans's personal qualities and delicately suggested that the controversial aspects of his career should be allowed to fade into the shadows.

Marcel Proust, writing the final volume of *A la recherche du temps perdu* not long after Constans's death, made brief mention of an ex-minister who had once been the object of criminal prosecution and intense public obloquy. With the passing of time, Proust wrote, old men died and memories faded; in the end, the politician lived to be honored and treated with deference. "For in fact no humiliation is so great that one should not accept it with unconcern, knowing that at the end of a few years our misdeeds will be no more than invisible dust. But time alone will achieve this result." Proust gave his character no name, but it is at least highly plausible that Constans's career was in his mind.

For most of his countrymen, Constans's name fell rapidly into complete and permanent eclipse. At most, there survived among historians and politicians the memory of his cleverness in tricking General Boulanger into ignominious flight, and thus presumably saving the republic. Perhaps it is just as well that posterity retains little else about him. Though many of his sins were undoubtedly exaggerated by his enemies, he will hardly serve as a textbook model of statesmanship and integrity for the young. Some cynics possess an inner core of idealism; Constans seems to have lacked that saving quality. He was a thoroughgoing cynic, protected against self-doubt by a rhinoceros-thick hide. No doubt he provides an extreme but revealing example of what a politician could get away with during the Third Republic. An American public figure of our day, under investigation for alleged ethical flaws and malfeasance in office, has been awkwardly described as "insensitive to the appearance of impropriety." In the end, perhaps that is the fairest judgment one can apply to Ernest Constans.

STEINLEN

9

Théophile Steinlen
Artist for the Masses

France lost its greatest caricaturist when Honoré Daumier died in 1879. Only two years later, a young Swiss artist arrived in Paris with a destiny which even he did not then suspect—to assume the Daumier succession.

Daumier's genius was not fully recognized until long after his time. He had amused or outraged his compatriots for almost a half-century with his savage depictions of politicians, bureaucrats, and businessmen, and his sympathetic or sardonic sketches of common people. He had been a vigorous partisan in the warfare between the powerful and the powerless, and his partisanship had gotten him into trouble repeatedly, even at times into prison. For his admirers outside the ruling élite, he was a heroic figure, a Saint George confronting the dragon of privilege or perhaps a modern-day Don Quixote. But his caricatures, most of which appeared in satirical weekly magazines, seemed too ephemeral to be taken seriously, while his oil paintings remained largely unknown until posterity discovered his greatness and placed him on the pedestal that he clearly deserved. Today, he has his room in the Musée d'Orsay.

Théophile Steinlen was somewhat more fortunate in that he achieved a considerable reputation during his lifetime. He was no mere imitator or shadow of Daumier, although the two artists had enough in common to encourage comparisons both then and later. Both of them were masters at delineating the popular life and mores of their times; both were unsparing satirists of the rich and mighty. Steinlen's work probably revealed a deeper sympathy than Daumier's for the victims of injustice in society, and his times allowed him greater freedom to criticize the powerful without much fear of retribution. Yet there is reason to think that Daumier in his heaven would not reject Steinlen as his artistic heir.

Steinlen, who always signed himself with only his family name, was born in Lausanne in 1859, the grandson of a German immigrant who had left Württemberg to escape the Napoleonic wars. Artistic talent ran in the family: Théophile's grandfather was a landscapist and teacher of drawing, and all but one of that patriarch's brood of ten children had some sort of artistic bent. The sole exception was Théophile's father, who had opted for a less romantic but more secure role as a postal employee. Théophile as a youngster roamed freely about the hills behind Lausanne; he had a passion for nature, and preferred collecting butterflies to dimming his sight in the classroom. His father sent him nevertheless to the University of Lausanne for two dilettantish years, at the end of which the parent lost patience and shipped him off to an uncle in Mulhouse to earn his living as a textile designer. Native talent revealed itself; he did well in his new employment.

Mulhouse, however, had little attraction for him. A small industrial city in Alsace was unlikely to provide much color and excitement for a young man barely past twenty. The mirage of Paris exerted a powerful attraction; his reading at the university had included some French novels, notably the shocking new best-seller *L'Assommoir* by Émile Zola, and while its portrayal of Parisian slum life was grim and oppressive rather than glamorous, it fascinated the young Swiss. No doubt it also stimulated his sympathy for the sufferings of working-class people, which so strongly marked his later artistic career. In any case, he set off in 1881 with his Alsatian girlfriend and eventual wife Emilie Mey, an apprentice dressmaker. Legend has it that they arrived with a single gold coin and a letter of introduction to a Montmartre painter; that when their money was gone, they sold or pawned their possessions piecemeal; and that they finally had to leave their cheap hotel near the scene of Zola's novel to sleep *al fresco* in the parks until he managed to find work, once again as a textile designer. There is a second version that is probably closer to the truth; it has him arriving from Mulhouse with a letter of recommendation from his uncle, addressed to a Paris colleague in the textile business, which made possible a less traumatic introduction to city life. He and Emilie settled into rooms in Montmartre, where they put down immediate and permanent roots. Both were to live out their remaining years—she until 1910 and he until 1923—in that freewheeling bohemian quarter.

Steinlen continued to show talent as a textile designer, but the work bored him; he was fascinated by the bustling street crowds of the quarter, and took to spending much of his time sketching ordinary people as they passed by his post of observation. His employer soon lost patience with his undisciplined performance, and put him on piecework pay—a change that made his life precarious. Luckily, a fellow Swiss introduced him to an unsuccessful artist named Rodolphe Salis who had just opened a small cabaret called Le Chat Noir; it provided drink and popular entertainment for the bohemian residents of the quarter. Salis soon added a little magazine to his expanding empire, and commissioned Steinlen to draw a stylized black cat as the magazine's logo. More important, the magazine provided Steinlen with the first outlet for his street sketches; and through friends whom he met at Le Chat Noir he was given other commissions. The cabaret caught on so well that Salis soon moved it to larger quarters, where it became one of the liveliest spots in Montmartre; artists, poets, singers congregated there, along with bourgeois revellers titillated by Montmartre's night life. Salis's former locale was taken over by the popular chansonnier Aristide Bruant, whose cabaret *Le Mirliton* soon surpassed its predecessor in notoriety. While Salis dressed his waiters in cast-off costumes of members of the Académie Française and greeted his guests with elaborate formality, Bruant specialized in insulting his customers and encouraging the raucous crowd to welcome newcomers with such chants as "Oh! la, la! what an ugly mug!" But it was Bruant's songs, written and sung by himself, that made him the most famous of Montmartre's performers. He became an enduring legend, and was eventually honored by the city with a street that bears his name. Bruant's dizzy rise gave Steinlen new opportunities; he became a regular contributor to Bruant's magazine *Le Mirliton*, and illustrated two highly successful volumes of Bruant's satirical song-poems. During off-hours, the two men roamed through the proletarian quarters of Paris in search of inspiration for songs and sketches.

Steinlen in the mid-1880s found still another outlet for his talents in that new popular art form, the poster. The development of color lithography and the relaxation of the city's rules on public advertising transformed the appearance of the Paris boulevards; brightly colored and artfully designed posters proliferated everywhere, proclaiming the virtues of everything from patent medicines and bicycles to theatrical performances and art exhibits. Steinlen quickly won recognition as one of the most effective poster artists; he developed a highly distinctive style that utilized solid blocks of bright color and simple, clear composition. His new prosperity enabled Steinlen to move his wife and daughter Colette into more spacious quarters at 58 rue Caulaincourt—the long street that winds up the flank of Montmartre. Christened "the Cat's Cottage," it was a small but picturesque *pavillon* with a garden that could house his remarkable collection of pets—including fifteen cats (one of them the model for Le Chat Noir), along with such exotics as a crocodile named Gustave. Nearby, at number 21, he rented a studio that had formerly been used by Toulouse-Lautrec.

All this might suggest that Steinlen, like so many other nine-

The First of May, 1894

teenth-century newcomers to Paris, was moving up from bare subsistence into the ranks of the cosseted bourgeoisie. Indeed, his life-
style did go through that kind of transition, but the evolution of
his political and social ideas as expressed in his art was carrying
him in quite the opposite direction. Steinlen's sympathies lay with
the ordinary people of Paris—construction workers, laundresses,
small shopkeepers, streetwalkers—who thronged the streets of
Montmartre and its northern slopes toward the Porte de Clignan-
court. During the 1880s, his drawings in the little magazines faithfully reflected the city's popular life and mores, but they contained
no hint of a social message. As time went by, however, they were
increasingly infused with a more explicitly humanitarian spirit, a
sense of community between the artist and his subjects. And by
the 1890s he had evolved into an outright social propagandist, issuing a blunt and angry challenge to the kind of state and society
that allowed such injustice and oppression. His drawings appeared

in a number of socialist, anarchist, and labor union organs; this work he often contributed gratis.

The rising intensity of Steinlen's sentiments mirrored the growth of social conflict in the last two decades of the century. Socialism in its various French forms was advancing steadily; almost fifty socialist deputies were elected to Parliament in 1893. The trade union movement, legalized in 1884, was adopting a more aggressive tone; its official doctrine of syndicalism favored the use of strikes and sabotage rather than parliamentary political action. Still more frightening to bourgeois Frenchmen was the sudden burst of anarchist terrorism that plagued Paris in the early 1890s. François Ravachol in 1891 planted bombs at the homes of law-and-order judges (Ravachol boasted at his trial that he had lost his Catholic faith as a youth by reading Sue's *Wandering Jew*). Auguste Vaillant in 1893 tossed a bomb from the gallery of the Chamber of Deputies onto the floor of Parliament; the presiding officer won brief renown by trumpeting, "Gentlemen, the session continues!" In 1894 a young Italian wielding a knife assassinated the president of the republic, Sadi Carnot.

Steinlen often turned up, sketch pad in hand, to record scenes of public disorder—demonstrations, strikes, clashes with the police. Although he was often categorized as an anarchist, he had little sympathy for the terrorist wing of the movement, which advocated and practiced what it called "propaganda by the deed." He was attracted rather to the ideas of such anarchist theoreticians as Peter Kropotkin, who preached a beatific doctrine of peace and brotherhood, a harmonious community of men and women free of all external compulsion. At the same time, he developed a friendly relationship with such Socialist notables as Jean Jaurès and Alexandre Millerand. But he avoided a formal commitment to any political movement; ideologically, he was a free-floater in that undefined zone where anarchism, socialism, and humanitarianism met and overlapped. His angry rejection of the bourgeois republic and of the capitalist "exploiters" reached its climax in the mid-1890s. In a series of crudely propagandistic drawings for *Le Chambard Socialiste*, he flayed the bourgeois regime for its social iniquities. One of these drawings portrayed the republican symbol Marianne on the arm of a fat bourgeois: two outraged workingmen shout, "Get lost, slut! you make us ashamed!" At the turn of the century, Steinlen became a leading contributor to the most widely read satirical magazine of the day, *L'Assiette au Beurre*, where he broadened his attack to include militarists, clericals, colonial imperialists, and parliamentary politicians in general. He also plunged into the Dreyfus affair, which reached a violent climax in 1898–99; along with most of the avant-garde writers and artists of Montmartre, he crusaded actively for a new trial for Captain Dreyfus. His commitment to that cause strengthened his friendship with such active Dreyfusards as Anatole France and Emile Zola.

Street Scene, c. 1900

The decade of the 1890s not only radicalized Steinlen, but also established him as one of the most widely known illustrators of his time. He contributed at some point in his career to fifty-six magazines, most of them Parisian. His work was in such demand that it left him little time for leisure or for social life; he was virtually chained to his drawing board. His reputation spread beyond France to the rest of Europe and even to the United States. Invitations came in 1894 to visit Germany and Norway; he spent six months there in his only long stay abroad. Aspiring young artists who arrived in Paris eagerly sought him out. Pablo Picasso recalled that when he first came to Paris in 1900, Steinlen's drawings and posters seemed to be everywhere he turned; some of Picasso's early work reflected Steinlen's influence. Käthe Kollwitz, planning her initial journey to the City of Light, placed Auguste Rodin and Steinlen at the head of her list of monuments to visit. After her meeting with Steinlen, she wrote admiringly but somewhat inaccurately: "He was a typical Parisian. The loose tobacco in his wide pants pockets, his continual rolling of cigarettes, his wife, his many children—all combined to produce a Parisian atmosphere." In fact, he had only one child, a daughter. The American-born artist Edward Hopper obviously absorbed some of the Steinlenian techniques during his Paris stay. And the Paris-born Georges Braque later claimed that his first childhood lesssons in art had come from copying Steinlen's drawings in the periodical *Gil Blas*.

With prosperity came more of the comforts of bourgeois existence, even though they were quite out of harmony with his increasingly radical social views. Although he denounced the republic, he chose in 1901 to abandon his Swiss roots and to adopt French citizenship. When his somewhat ramshackle "Cat's Cottage" was demolished to make way for a modern building, he found a comfortable new apartment up the street at number 73. Like any good bourgeois Parisian, he was to remain settled there for the rest of his life, and after his death the apartment was inherited by his daughter and his niece. Steinlen also acquired a small suburban *pavillon* where he could putter in the garden on weekends and engage in his new passion for oil painting. He saw himself always, however, as an illustrator rather than a serious painter, even though at his death he left some two hundred canvases. He clung to traditional techniques, largely ignoring the various experimental currents that were running so strongly in the Paris of his time. When galleries in Paris staged exhibitions of his work, as they did for the first time in 1894 and again in 1903, he chose to show only his drawings and engravings. His interest lay in the content and message of his work; his goal was not to see it displayed in a museum, but rather to arouse an emotional response among his fellow Parisians, to persuade them that the world must be changed.

Steinlen's friends claimed to find in him a kind of saintly quality, revealed in his deep humanitarianism and in his optimistic conviction that poverty and oppression could be conquered. Yet some scholars have found in his character one serious flaw—a strain of anti-Semitism. The evidence for such a charge is, however, shaky. It is true that his caricatures of fat cigar-chomping tycoons were sometimes portrayed with the prominent hooked nose that was often used to symbolize the Jewish banker. It is true also that the socialist and trade union movements in the 1890s were inclined to link capitalism and the Jews; at some trade union conventions, notorious anti-Semites were invited as featured speakers. In Steinlen's case, the accusation is therefore plausible, but no more than that. His energetic defense of Captain Dreyfus is effective evidence against the charge.

Although Steinlen continued after 1900 to contribute to the periodical press (one careful scholar has counted more than two thousand such drawings during his career), he now diverted more of his energy to illustrating limited-edition books: works by Anatole France and Maupassant, for example, and a cover design for his friend Zola's novel *Paris*. He chose books with a social message, and he continued to draw inspiration from the reality of life about him. To prepare the illustrations for Émile Morel's *Les gueules noires*, he

Colonization, 1902

spent time in a coal-mining town in the north, sketching and talking to miners; for another project, he visited the women's prison of Saint-Lazare in Paris. The outbreak of the Great War, however, altered his vision somewhat. For a time his drawings showed an unexpected touch of patriotic fervor, exalting the French cause as a struggle for liberty against German militarism. But as the conflict dragged on, a gloomier spirit suffused his work; where he had once seen poverty and oppression as the sources of human misery, now that source was war itself. Steinlen's wartime drawings have sometimes been compared, in their dark tones and their grim subject matter, to those of Goya: exhausted soldiers, Belgian families driven from their homes by the Germans, French women and children fleeing their smashed cities. This dark mood was to persist in his drawings of the postwar period; the earlier vision of a brighter future seemed to give way to a sense of uncertainty and even despair. That uncharacteristic pessimism was not Steinlen's alone; it reflected the devastating impact of the war on many European intellectuals.

For a half-century after his death in 1923, Steinlen's fame went into eclipse. As in the case of Daumier, most of his work seemed ephemeral, confined as it was to the pages of the popular press. Steinlen's resurgence in popular esteem took longer than in the case of Daumier, but recognition came at last in the 1970s. No doubt it was stimulated in part by the surge of social protest that marked the era; to many of the protesters, Steinlen seemed a kindred spirit. Steinlen's friend Anatole France had once said of his work that it possessed "a terrible simplicity"—that it was therefore self-explanatory, easily accessible to any viewer. Perhaps that quality makes it timeless as well. But it was also firmly rooted in its time, in those years from the 1880s to 1914 when prosperity and privation existed side by side in France, and the tension between them heightened. As Emile Zola had done in the novel, Steinlen caught and preserved his world of proletarian Paris, the seamy side of the *belle époque*.

10

Charles Péguy
Ambiguous Icon

In September 1914, on the first day of the battle of the Marne, a patriotic icon was born. Fifteen miles from Paris in a field of sugarbeets, an overage French infantry lieutenant fell mortally wounded, his forehead pierced by a German bullet. He had been the last surviving officer of his company; as emergency commander, he had stood erect directing the fire of his few remaining men until the bullet found its mark. The next morning the French armies launched the counterattack that drove the invaders back some sixty miles. Paris was saved by the "miracle" of the Marne.

Charles Péguy's heroic death at the outset of the great battle brought him the kind of glory for which he had long thirsted. Until then he had been unknown to the vast majority of his countrymen; now he was exalted as a martyr to the defense of the motherland and to the cause of civilization. As the first French casualty of the Great War with some claim to intellectual eminence, his death had a special resonance. His sacrifice was made even more poignant by the fact that at the age of forty-one, he had refused the normal assignment to a rear-echelon post and had volunteered for active front-line duty. Besides, this intellectual was a man of the people, son of a widowed mother who earned her living as a humble mender of cane chairs. His prewar writings had been suffused with patriotic and religious emotion: paeans of praise for Joan of Arc, lyrical passages of love for *la patrie*, and evidence of a deep and mystical Catholic faith. All the elements were present for the elevation of Charles Péguy to iconhood.

The long strain of the Great War increased France's need for heroes. Publishers brought out small volumes of selections from Péguy's writings, which served admirably to raise the nation's spirits during the dark periods of deadlock at the front, and to inspire young *lycéens* waiting to join the fight. Victory in 1918 brought a first apotheosis; the government posthumously awarded him the Legion of Honor, fulfilling an ambition for formal recognition that had remained frustrated throughout the prewar years. During the twenties and thirties, the Péguy legend was further embellished by hagiographic memoirs published by some of his old friends. Nationalists recruited him to counter the rise of pacifism and defeatism in a nation exhausted by the bloodletting of the war; Catholic dignitaries extolled him as a shining example of the resurgence of belief. But the real burst of interest in Péguy came after France's defeat in 1940, and in the course of the long subsequent quest for national resurrection and renewal. He was immediately claimed both by adherents of Marshal Pétain's Vichy regime and by Charles de Gaulle's Free French movement in London. Vichyite conservatives, and even some advocates of a French version of national socialism, looked to him as a sympathizer; Péguy's eldest son Marcel assured them that his father would undoubtedly have been on their side. Marcel said proudly that his father had been "above all, a racist." Meanwhile, Free French broadcasters read passages from his works to raise the morale of the underground forces, and General de Gaulle himself was said to keep a volume by Péguy on his bedside table. No matter who won this Franco-French war, Péguy seemed destined to emerge with his icon status further enhanced.

That destiny was indeed fulfilled. The postwar decades brought Péguy the kind of recognition that had steadily been denied him in his lifetime. Scholarly studies of Péguy's life and writings have become a minor industry in French universities and literary circles. His complete works have been published in three stout volumes, supplemented by bulky collections of hitherto unpublished essays and poetry. The Sorbonne, which he vilified unceasingly, staged an impressive ceremony in his honor. A *Centre Charles Péguy* (archive and museum) has been established in his native Orléans. Each year a pilgrimage of Catholic students from Paris to Chartres cathedral, a hundred-mile round trip on foot, replicates Péguy's legendary pilgrimage of 1912, which fulfilled his vow to the Virgin when his son recovered from a grave illness. In 1967, 20,000 young Catholics participated in this rite. Since 1973, his centennial year, a small monument stands near the cathedral's entrance, bearing his sculptured image and a verse from one of his poems to the glory of Chartres.

Charles Péguy's stature and permanence among the national icons of France thus seems to be assured. One question remains, however: has the man become obscured by the myth? Has legend created a Péguy who bears little relation to the living person, once brought down from his pedestal? A few critics have already suggested as much; and many aspects of Péguy's troubled, unhappy life lend considerable support to their doubts. At the very least, he was a man of great psychological complexity, who fits uneasily into the simplified two-dimensional image of a standard icon. Perhaps that is not surprising. Of many established saints, the same thing might be said.

* * *

Péguy's roots are found in the common people of central France: peasants, working-class folk. Born in 1873 in a suburb of Orléans, he was brought up in poverty by his widowed mother and his grandmother. His father, a veteran of the Franco-Prussian war, died when the child was less than a year old. Madame Veuve Péguy was a hard-driving woman who was determined to see her son succeed in life. When her husband died, she learned the chair-mending trade and later supplemented her income by opening a small grocery store and bar in her home. Her earnings eventually permitted her to become a property owner; she acquired several small rental houses, income from which enabled her to supplement her son's partial scholarship. In her somewhat tyrannical household there seems to have been little room for warmth and affection. Charles was a dutiful child, regular in his church observance, conscientious and talented in school. From the outset, his intellectual gifts impressed his teachers, who arranged for his admission to the Orléans *lycée*. A proletarian child among bourgeois schoolmates, he overcame the effects of class prejudice by his phenomenal performance. He emerged at the top of his class, with honors in subjects ranging from French composition to the natural sciences. He was also the star performer on the *lycée's* soccer team, which he helped to organize. Charles's parish priest attempted to recruit him for the seminary, but without success. He had already struck up a friendship with a self-educated blacksmith who professed socialist convictions of the pre-Marxian sort. Jean Boitier's influence evidently sufficed to counteract priestly pressure and maternal wishes.

Péguy's *lycée* teachers anticipated a brilliant academic future for their star pupil. Their goal was to see him admitted to the École Normale Superieure in Paris, which had become a kind of hothouse for nurturing the Third Republic's professional and teaching élite. Admission to Normale usually required a year or two of preparatory cramming. For that purpose, his sponsors obtained a partial scholarship at a *lycée* in the Paris suburbs. Péguy continued to perform brilliantly, yet the year ended in his first disappointment; he failed Normale's entrance examination by a half-point (62½ instead of 63). Before continuing for a second cram year, he decided to take time out for his compulsory military service. A new law permitted sons of widows to abbreviate their service from three years to one; Péguy took advantage of that option. For the first but not the last time, he showed his skill in what later came to be called *système D*—i.e., evading the formal bureaucratic regulations by finding some kind of loophole. After his year in the barracks, he returned in 1893–94 to the cramming routine, this time at the Collège Sainte-Barbe and the Lycée Louis-le-Grand in the Latin quarter. There he found a circle of classmates who remained his close friends thereafter, although most of Péguy's friendships, these included, ended sooner or later in conflict and alienation. This time the cramming was effective; he was ranked an impressive sixth in Normale's entrance examination, and was thus assured of three years of élite training with all expenses paid. At the end lay the *agrégation* examination, success in which would qualify him for a post as *lycée* professor, and with luck, an eventual university chair.

Before that day of academic harvest arrived, however, Péguy's path had begun to diverge from what had heretofore been a pattern of conformity and almost unbroken success. Two fateful decisions marked his years at Normale. The first was his "conversion" (his word) to socialism. Lucien Herr, the librarian at Normale, had galvanized some of the liveliest students into a socialist study group; Herr's influence was supplemented by that of Jean Jaurès, a recent Normale graduate who was emerging as leader of the socialist bloc in Parliament. Péguy was a ready recruit; he became an enthusiastic participant.

For young socialists, these were heady times; they were buoyed by the belief that France and the western world were on the verge of a profound transformation that would convert the selfish bourgeois system into a harmonious socialist commonwealth. Although the French socialist movement was riven by factionalism, it was growing faster than any rival force, and the high-minded idealism and oratorical brilliance of Jaurès gave his admirers the conviction that their champion was supremely equipped to lead the country. Péguy came under Jaurès's spell, and for the first time neglected his studies to engage in militant activism. He wrote articles for the socialist press, organized a study circle in Orléans, and set out to combine his literary and political interests by writing a play about the life of Joan of Arc, in which the villains would be the spineless king and the hypocritical churchmen who ordered Joan's execution. Implicitly, the play would convey his new socialist outlook. To gain time for writing, Péguy resorted again to *système D*; pleading eye trouble and headaches, he obtained a series of leaves of absence from Normale that lasted throughout his second year there. When he returned in 1896 to make up that second year, he continued to spend most of his time completing his Joan of Arc.

By this time he had made a second decision, even more fundamental to his future. Instead of becoming a teacher, he would make a career as a writer whose influence would speed the transformation of the world while at the same time winning him personal glory. He was determined now to remain in Paris, where the action was, and avoid "immolation" (as he put it) in some dismal provincial town. But how could he honorably escape that fate? By *système D* once more; if he married, he would be required to resign from Normale. As his bride he chose eighteen-year-old Charlotte Baudouin, sister of his closest friend from *lycée* days, who had recently died of typhoid fever. His new wife and her family were dedicated freethinkers and anticlericals who found Péguy's socialist ideas congenial; a substantial dowry accompanied the bride. Péguy duly resigned from Normale, but his expertise in the practice of *système D* enabled him to retain his scholarship and to audit some courses designed to prepare him for the *agrégation*. But when examination day came in 1898 he failed dismally, to the shock of his friends and the outrage of his mother, who was already furious at his marriage to an unbeliever. The suspicion that Péguy expected and intended to fail is hard to avoid, for he had neglected his courses at Normale and had told friends that he would never accept provincial exile. Although he might have tried for the *agrégation* again a year or so later, he never did so. It was a surprising end to an academic career that had begun so brilliantly; and in retrospect one can see it as a crucial turning point in his life.

At the moment, Péguy showed no disappointment, but only re-lief. He was already vigorously engaged in more exciting activities. The Dreyfus affair was one of them; it reached its climax in the years from 1897 to 1900. Péguy followed Jaurès into his campaign for a new trial for Dreyfus, rejecting the stance of many socialists that it was merely a squabble between bourgeois factions. For Péguy as for Jaurès, it was a true moral crusade on behalf of justice and humanity—a crusade to defend an individual who had been wronged by bigoted oppressors. He took part in street demonstra-tions, and at the Sorbonne joined students who were defending Dreyfusard professors against attack. Péguy was even more busily engaged in a second venture: the establishment of a bookstore and publishing house that would serve the socialist cause. This enter-prise, at 17 rue Cujas in the Latin quarter, was launched by in-vesting the entire dowry of 40,000 francs brought by his wife. It failed disastrously. At the end of a year, the operation faced bank-ruptcy; indeed, it was 75,000 francs in debt, and Péguy faced possible prosecution. He made a desperate appeal to his socialist friends at Normale, and they came to his rescue. Herr and his young disciple Léon Blum contributed sizable sums to bail Péguy out, and reorganized the business to ensure against a repetition. They managed to salvage more than half of Péguy's investment, but he had to give up control to a board of five headed by Herr. Péguy's pride was hurt; he soon resigned from the firm in a fury, denounc-ing the friends who had tried to protect his interests. A bitter dispute over the firm's assets followed, ending at last in the courts. Péguy posed as the innocent victim of grasping schemers, and lost no opportunity thereafter to vilify Herr and his circle. It was hardly a promising start for his new nonacademic career.

Péguy meanwhile had embarked on a second publishing venture, this time with somewhat greater success. He became the editor of a new semimonthly periodical called *Cahiers de la Quinzaine* whose declared purpose was to publish important socialist texts and news of the socialist movement. The enterprise soon settled in at 8 rue de la Sorbonne, across the street from the university. In these spartan quarters, and with little help save one assistant and occasional volunteers, Péguy managed to keep the *Cahiers* alive from 1900 to 1914, and to publish a total of 229 issues. Their original purpose, however, was soon forgotten, as Péguy's commitment to socialism faded. The *Cahiers* published a mélange of essays and fiction—notably Romain Rolland's novel *Jean-Christophe*—but above all they became the outlet for Péguy's own essays and poems. The *Cahiers* survived precariously from the outset; there were barely enough subscribers to keep it afloat, and Péguy had to expend much of his energy badgering his readers to continue their subscriptions. That became increasingly difficult as Péguy's evolution to the right alienated many of his initial subscribers, who had come mainly from the left. To keep the magazine alive, Péguy had to soft-pedal the public expression of his new beliefs. For a man of such strong convictions, this must have caused considerable psychological stress. And added stress was surely what he did not need. He complained incessantly to his friends of overwork and exhaustion, of inability to provide for his growing family, of lack of appreciation for his sacrifices. At times he was ready to give up in despair, and to face the grim prospect of a teaching career far from Paris. With this in mind, he registered a thesis topic for the doctorate at the Sorbonne, and actually wrote almost two hundred pages before abandoning that effort. Throughout the decade, his morale went through such violent swings from euphoria to black depression that one is tempted to diagnose him as mildly manic-depressive.

When and why was this young socialist intellectual transformed into an exponent of emotional nationalism and reconverted to a mystical Catholicism? The answer is far from simple. There seems to have been no sudden change, no incident of the born-again variety; the process occurred gradually from 1900 onward. Several factors contributed to his disillusionment with socialism. There was his anger at Herr and others after the failure of his publishing venture. There was his bitterness at being rejected as a delegate to the socialist unity congress in 1900, where he had fantasized a starring role for himself. And there was his belief that the leaders of socialism—notably Jaurès—were selling out their noble humanitarian ideals in order to further their selfish political ambitions. The young Péguy had been an enthusiastic disciple in Jaurès's crusade on behalf of Captain Dreyfus; he had admired the great tribune with real passion. But when Jaurès then proceeded to make political compromises in an effort to unify the socialist factions and to defend the republic against its enemies, Péguy was outraged. He refused to understand why Jaurès brought the socialists into an informal coalition with the bourgeois Radicals, whom he regarded as venal opportunists. He denounced the Radical government's anticlerical measures—the exile of most religious orders and the separation of church and state. For Péguy, men who had fought against the persecution of Dreyfus had become the new persecutors, with the innocent Catholics as their victims. High-minded idealism, he complained, had been abandoned in favor of low-minded self-seeking; in his phrase, *mystique* had given way to *politique*.

The strain of fanaticism in Péguy's character now began to emerge more strongly; he could not tolerate the kind of compromises essential in democratic politics. His refusal to try to understand the rationale for Jaurès's conduct led him into a campaign of vituperation and distortion that continually intensified until it reached the level of obsessive frenzy. Jaurès, he wrote, was a demagogue, a hypocrite, a coward, a knave, a tyrannical satrap, a false intellectual, a German agent seeking to sell out France to the enemy. He apologized to his readers for mentioning Jaurès's name— "a name so contemptibly filthy that printing it may subject me to some penal law." By 1913 he was ready to suggest that if war broke out, Jaurès should be guillotined. He is alleged to have "exulted like a schoolboy" at the news of Jaurès's assassination in July 1914. That he really did so has been disputed; but it is clear that he expressed no regret at the murder of his onetime idol. Jaurès met the torrent of vilification with patient forebearance; his only response was to let his subscription to the *Cahiers* lapse.

If Jaurès was the principal target of Péguy's invective, he was not alone. Péguy used his talent as pamphleteer to settle accounts with his enemies, his "false friends," and those literary critics who failed to appreciate his writings. His collective targets were what he called "the intellectual party" and "the Sorbonne." The former label covered those writers and thinkers of the left who had been his masters or associates in his earlier socialist phase. "The Sorbonne" was a grab-bag designation for that segment of "the intellectual party"—especially sociologists and historians—whom he accused of monopolizing such prestigious positions as professorial chairs and membership in the learned academies, and whose pedestrian minds made them jealous and hostile toward anyone with true genius. Here again a kind of obsession moved him to repeated attacks on such notables as the historians Ernest Lavisse and Charles Langlois, whose scholarly honors and generous salaries Péguy openly envied.

Péguy's conversion to a superpatriotic line can be quite precisely dated. The Moroccan crisis of 1905 shocked him into a sense that France's security was threatened by a militaristic Germany. In his essay *Notre patrie* he trumpeted his commitment to a new chauvinism; he called for military preparedness and for alerting the nation to the imminence of war. His immediate reaction was to head for the Bon Marché, where he bought the equipment he would need on the battlefield; legend has it that he never unpacked his knapsack from that time until 1914. In his writings thereafter France was exalted as a mystic entity embodying all the virtues, and requiring the devotion of all her sons. Sometimes, but not often, his passion was leavened by a touch of irony:

> What a bore it will be, says God, when there are no more
> of these Frenchmen,
> I will do things, there will be nobody to understand
> them.

Péguy's return to a new form of his childhood Christian faith is more difficult to date. From 1905 onward, he dropped occasional hints of it in private conversations with friends, but he delayed any public expression of it until 1911. Some critics believe that he kept his silence to protect the *Cahiers* against the potentially fatal loss of his anticlerical subscribers. Eventually, however, he could delay no longer; his renewed faith found open expression in his essays and especially in his poetry. Beginning in 1910, he embarked on a series of long poems about Joan of Arc, but in a quite different spirit from that which had marked his earlier work about Joan. This time the clergy were no longer the villains; Joan had become the embodiment of the highest Christian virtues, and the patroness of the French "race." With these poems, it seemed for a time that Péguy had finally found an admiring audience. *Le mystère de la charité de Jeanne d'Arc* was reviewed and warmly praised in the conservative and Catholic press; Péguy basked in the acclaim, and felt that his long isolation had ended. For a time his mood was altered; in place of the recurrent self-doubt and mild paranoia that had haunted him for years, a burst of hope and confidence transformed his outlook. He saw himself as a future member of the Académie Française, and was encouraged to think that he might aspire to the Académie's 1911 grand prize, which would not only give him financial security but would guarantee his future literary success. To improve his chances he published a volume of his selected writings, which had gone unnoticed in the *Cahiers*. In his passion to win the award, Péguy sought to mobilize every possible acquaintance who might influence the Académie's vote; his campaign involved the kind of shamelessly obsequious appeals that he had always denounced with contempt. Alas, it all proved to be useless; the Academicians deadlocked between his candidacy and that of Romain Rolland, and ended by making no award. Even though they voted him a lesser prize as a kind of consolation, Péguy was both devastated and furious. His supposed friends, he claimed, had failed to back him strongly enough; his enemies, the "intellectual party" and "the Sorbonne," had conspired to defeat him. After the euphoria of 1910, he slipped once more into a mood of gloom and defeat.

Among the "false friends" who had failed to support him properly, Péguy numbered the eminent philosopher Henri Bergson. Péguy had been a Bergson disciple ever since his days at Normale, where Bergson taught for a time before winning a chair at the Collège de France. He faithfully attended Bergson's public lectures at the Collège, along with the crowd of Parisian socialites and left-bank intellectuals. The Bergsonian philosophy, with its stress on intuition over reason, on fluidity over rigidity, on *élan vital*, was congenial to Péguy; it may have been a factor in stimulating his mystical approach to religion, and it may have affected Péguy's literary style as well. His writing became increasingly prolix and repetitive, to the dismay of his longtime friends and of such readers as Marcel Proust. Himself no stranger to prolixity, Proust found Péguy's work "unreadable." Péguy badgered Bergson with requests to contribute an essay to the *Cahiers*, which would have been a major coup, but Bergson always managed to elude any commitment. Bergson's unwillingness to support Péguy for the Académie prize was an even more severe disappointment, yet for once Péguy did not react by breaking off relations and denouncing the offender. Bergson was one of the few to arouse Péguy's displeasure without being publicly condemned.

One curious aspect of the "new Péguy" was that his recovery of faith left him still outside the church. Even after Péguy publicly disclosed his reconversion, he never entered a church to hear mass or to receive the sacraments. Indeed, he continued to express private criticism of the clergy, and to blame them for dechristianizing France. Like the socialist leaders, the priests were accused of abandoning *mystique* for *politique*—of forgetting true Christian ideals in the rush to play the political game. Péguy's admirers have found an excuse for his unorthodox behavior in the fact that his civil marriage to an unbeliever and his failure to have his children baptized made it impossible for him to participate in church rituals unless he could persuade his wife to return to the faith. This he could not or would not do, out of respect for her autonomy of decision. Perhaps this painful situation does explain and justify his conduct. Yet his continuing anticlerical remarks suggest that his mystical conception of man's relation to God required no intercession by a churchly institution. If so, his aloofness from the church may have involved no great sacrifice on his part.

If the formal consolations of religion were denied to Péguy, the more intimate consolations of domesticity had never amounted to much in his unhappy, even tortured, existence. There had never been much warmth in the couple's conjugal relations, and domestic harmony was not improved by his straitened financial circumstances. Péguy complained often about the burdens of raising a family—three children by 1903, a fourth on the way at the time of his death. He confided less often to his friends about the increased alienation of his wife and his mother-in-law over his return to the faith. They stood fast in their positivist and anticlerical convictions, and must have resented what they saw as Péguy's "apostasy." Péguy's mother further exacerbated his personal problems; she was never reconciled to his marriage and felt betrayed by his failure to justify her sacrifices by attaining a prestigious academic post. Péguy moved his household in 1899 from Paris to a suburban semi-rural retreat, from which he commuted via the new Sceaux rail line. On the surface, the family seemed to enjoy an idyllic existence there, with a dog, three cats, and two goats to entertain the children. The latter were taught at home by their parents, at least until the final years of *lycée*; the oldest son Marcel failed his *bachot*, which led Péguy to blame his Sorbonnard enemies for having conspired (again!) to persecute him via his son.

A few durable friendships provided him some solace. Thursday luncheons at the apartment of Madame Geneviève Favre, daughter of the eminent statesman Jules Favre and mother of Jacques Maritain, offered the best opportunity for brief escape and relaxation; two young men, Maritain and Maurice Reclus (civil servant and biographer) were the other regulars. On Thursday afternoons the *Cahiers* office was the venue for a group of intimates who gathered for a freewheeling discussion of ideas and politics; for several years, until the usual falling-out, the iconoclastic political theorist Georges Sorel was the dominant presence, pontificating at length, and accompanying Péguy to the Bergson lectures. Péguy struck up a new friendship in 1909 with a wealthy and worldly couple, Claude Casimir-Périer and his actress wife Simone; he took to spending considerable time at their chateau outside Paris, where he rubbed elbows with the city's social élite. This indulgence offended some of Péguy's old acquaintances, who remembered his former contempt for social climbers. But at least he did not try to match the elegance of his new friends; even in the Casimir-Périer salon, he continued to dress in his careless bohemian fashion—broad-brimmed felt hat, artist's-style cape, stout workman's shoes. Simone later remembered him as resembling "a little village schoolmaster."

Into this life of unremitting labor and general frustration, one touch of romance did intrude. Only two or three of Péguy's most trusted friends knew of it at the time; it was unsuspected by biographers for a generation, and is still treated with gingerly caution by most Péguy critics. Péguy met Blanche Raphael, a young Jewish student pursuing the *agrégation* in English, in 1902 or 1903. She was the sister of one of the contributors to the *Cahiers*, and seems to have done a bit of volunteer work there. Blanche was five years younger than Péguy—attractive, lively, "*très flirt*," as one acquaintance put it. Péguy's passionate attachment to her seems to have begun around 1905, though whether she knew then or later of the intensity of his feelings is not clear. For him it was apparently the great love, the only love, of his life; and his moral scruples forced him to live for years with the frustrations of an unfulfilled love. In 1910 Blanche married a young man of no means and not much promise; Péguy encouraged the match, apparently in the hope that a formal barrier between them might end his obsession. If so, it failed; he remained tormented by her loss, provided some funds from his own limited resources to keep the ménage going, and in August 1914 wrote to her frequently from the front until his death in battle. Blanche had once expressed regret that she could do nothing to repay his kindnesses; he had answered, "You have made me a poet." Her inspiration seems to have been the major impulse behind Péguy's turn from prose to poetry during the years from 1910 onward, when he wrote with a kind of frenzied energy and produced some of his most admired works. But if his romantic passion gave an impulse to his creativity, it must have added still further to the psychological stresses of his last years.

Since 1905, Péguy had been ready and eager for what he believed to be an inevitable and necessary war. On August 2, 1914, he said his farewells to wife and children and went off to Paris for his last two days before reporting for duty. He spent the nights on a sofa at Madame Favre's and the days visiting many of the old friends with whom he had broken off relations in years past. He wanted, he said, to leave with the clear conscience that he had patched up all the old hatreds. His regiment was sent directly to the frontier, in Lorraine; but before much action occurred there, all units had to be hastily withdrawn to help defend Paris against the German armies crunching through Belgium and northern France. Both legend and fact, insofar as we can know it, show him to have been an excellent soldier and an exceptional officer. The war, it seemed, had freed him of his demons and had provided him with a sense of destiny. He welcomed the challenge, and rose to it. How often thereafter were Péguy's admirers to quote his own lines, and to suggest that they were prophetic:

Heureux ceux qui sont morts pour la terre charnelle,
Mais pourvu que ce fut dans une juste guerre.
Heureux ceux qui sont morts pour quatre coins de terre.
Heureux ceux qui sont morts d'une mort solennelle.

Heureux ceux qui sont morts dans les grandes batailles,
Couchés dessus le sol à la face de Dieu.
Heureux ceux qui sont morts sur un dernier haut lieu,
Parmi tout l'appareil des grandes funerailles.*

Péguy would hardly have become a national icon if he had not died at such a moment, and so dramatically. Chance often makes a large contribution to sorting out the famous from the forgotten. French patriots, both during the Great War and again after the 1940 disaster, needed an exemplary figure whose impassioned rhetoric and ultimate sacrifice could be used to bolster the nation's resolve. Charles Péguy served that need—and chance served his legend well.

---

*Freely translated, these verses might read thus:
 Happy are they who die for their native soil,
 But only if they find death in a just war.
 Happy are they who die for their small patch of earth.
 Happy are they who die a ceremonious death.

 Happy are they who die at the battlefront
 Stretched out on the earth's face in the sight of God.
 Happy are they who die on a last high place,
 And are borne in funereal pomp to their final rest.

Postscript

At the end of this guided tour through nineteenth-century Paris, do any useful generalizations emerge? Is there some pervasive principle, some theme that ties the ten lives together and gives coherence to this book?

A number of linkages did turn up, unanticipated at the outset. Delphine Gay, for example, was a longtime acquaintance of Eugène Sue, and was involved late in life with Allan Kardec's spiritism. Juliette Adam knew Delphine's husband Emile de Girardin; she met, and detested, Clémence Royer; she encountered, and liked, the young Marquis de Morès; and she once invited Ernest Constans to dinner; he failed to show up, and apologized. Constans blocked Morès's business schemes in Indo-China; Morès sought revenge by campaigning against Constans's reelection to Parliament. These links suggest that Paris, or the part of it I have chosen to study, had something of the qualities of a small town. They suggest too that Parisian social and intellectual clans, then as now, were exclusive but somewhat permeable; there was a tendency for circles to overlap.

These personal links, however, do not suffice to provide an integrating principle. Two other generalizations carry more weight. First, all but two of the ten characters sketched were of bourgeois origin; the exceptions were the aristocrat Morès and the proletarian Péguy. Second, only two of the ten, Morès and Sue, were Paris-born.

My choice of bourgeois protagonists who had emigrated from the provinces was not intentional, but it did grow naturally out of the structure of nineteenth-century Parisian life. Whether or not the Great Revolution of 1789 was a bourgeois revolution—and learned scholars now are skeptical—it did open the way to a bourgeois century. In successive stages, new strata of the population found it possible to move up into the élite or the sub-élite, where they could share at least some of the advantages of status and power. Birth and wealth continued to count heavily, especially until mid-century; but by 1900 the middle classes had staked out important territory in business, the state bureaucracy, and parliamentary politics. A sociological X-ray of the city's population would of course have provided greater attention to the working class and to women. But my purpose was to focus on a series of intriguing characters who won some degree of eminence in their time. Most of those Parisians who broke the surface and became famous for fifteen minutes were in the nature of things both bourgeois and male. Neither women nor proletarians had an equivalent chance in that era to emerge into public notice. A century that is bourgeois and male-dominated is likely to produce male bourgeois notables.

Still, why should only two of the chosen ten be Paris-born? This too may be less anomalous than one might think. The influx of Parisians into Paris during the nineteenth century was enormous; the city's population grew from a little over a half-million to almost three million, and most of that increase came through migration rather than natural growth. Furthermore, statistical studies by the historian Adeline Daumard have shown that provincial migrants outpaced native Parisians in clawing their way up the ladder of success. Evidently they were more energetic, more highly motivated; perhaps many Parisian natives had settled back into a satisfied comfort that left the newcomers more space to operate.

A varied gallery of characters provides a series of different windows into the kaleidoscopic reality of nineteenth-century Parisian life. The eminent Oxford philosopher Isaiah Berlin has reminded us that historians come in two models—the hedgehog and the fox. Foxes, he observes, know many things but hedgehogs know one big thing. Hedgehog-historians insist on seeking out one overarching principle into which everything must fit, while fox-historians are fascinated by the rich variety that marks humanity's past. Nineteenth-century Paris, I believe, lends itself better to the fox's view than to the hedgehog's. It is a perspective that I share by instinct; and in the end it explains the content and shape of this book.

Acknowledgments

A book of essays such as this requires no extensive bibliography. I do wish, however, to express my debt to the authors of several biographical works on which I have drawn for factual information, although I have not always shared their interpretation of the facts.

Delphine Gay de Girardin has inspired no adequate biography, but two studies of her husband's career help to fill the gap: Maurice Reclus, *Emile de Girardin, le créateur de la presse moderne* (Paris: Hachette, 1934), and Pierre Pellissier, *Emile de Girardin, prince de la presse* (Paris: Hachette, 1985).

On Eugène Sue: Jean-Louis Bory, *Eugène Sue* (Paris: Hachette, 1978).

On Allan Kardec: Jean Vartier, *Allan Kardec, la naissance du spiritisme* (Paris: Hachette, 1971).

On Clémence Royer: Geneviève Fraisse, *Clémence Royer, philosophe et femme de sciences* (Paris: La Découverte, 1985).

On Juliette Adam: Saad Morcos, *Juliette Adam* (Cairo: Dar Al-Maaref, 1961).

145

On the Marquis de Morès: Charles Droulers, *Le Marquis de Morès, 1858–1896* (Paris: Plon, 1932) on his career in France; and Donald Dresden, *The Marquis de Morès, Emperor of the Bad Lands* (Norman, Okla.: Univ. of Oklahoma Press, 1970), on his Dakota adventure.

On Diana Vaughan and her creator Léo Taxil: Eugen Weber, *Satan Franc-Maçon* (Paris: René Julliard, 1964).

On Théophile Steinlen: Maurice Pianzola, *Théophile-Alexandre Steinlen* (Lausanne: ed. Rencontre, 1971), and Phillip D. Cate and Susan Gill, *Théophile-Alexandre Steinlen* (G. M. Smith: Salt Lake City, 1982).

On Charles Péguy: Henri Guillemin, *Charles Péguy* (Paris: Seuil, 1981). Guillemin's is the most detailed of the many books on Péguy; it is also the most critical. Other informative studies include those by Marjorie Villiers, Hans A. Schmitt, André Robinet, and Julie Sabiani.

Various Parisians who crossed paths with the figures in this book have left amusing sidelights in their memoirs or journals—notably Edmond and Jules de Goncourt, *Journal: mémoires de la vie littéraire* (Monaco: Imprimerie nationale, 1956–58, 22 vol.); and Comtesse Marie d'Agoult, *Mes souvenirs 1806–1833* (Paris: Calmann-Lévy, 1880), and *Mémoires 1833–1854* (Paris: Calmann-Lévy, 1927).

Seven of the ten subjects sketched in these essays were themselves prolific authors; I have drawn extensively but selectively on their writings. The exceptions were Steinlen, who used his pen in a different way, and Morès and Constans, who were not inclined to put anything on paper. Rather surprisingly, only two of the ten wrote memoirs or autobiographies. Juliette Adam published seven rather self-serving volumes covering the first half of her career; Clémence Royer left a handwritten memoir of ninety pages, plus a supplementary note of five pages about her relationship with Pascal Duprat. Both of these documents are preserved in the Bibliothèque Marguerite Durand.

Ernest Constans remains the most elusive figure among the ten— a curious fact, given his role as a public figure. No biographer has risked the encounter with so slippery a personality; most historians of the period have preferred to leave him in limbo, except for his role in the Boulanger crisis. There is a savagely hostile account in Alexandre Zévaès's *Henri Rochefort, le pamphletaire* (Paris: E.F.E., 1946), and his ambassadorial career is treated episodically in Jacques Thobie's massive monograph *Intérëts et impérialisme français dans l'empire ottoman* (Paris: Imprimerie Nationale, 1977). Many of Constans's despatches from Constantinople appear in the multivolume *Documents Diplomatiques Français 1871–1914*, published by the Ministère des Affaires Estrangères. Constans's private papers in the archives of that ministry contain nothing of interest. In fact, the most revealing source on Constans is the huge file of clippings and police reports in the archives of the Prefecture of Police. Those archives also contain extensive material on Morès and Taxil, and some details on Clémence Royer and her *amant* Pascal Duprat.

The illustrations in this book come from the collections of the Bibliothèque Nationale or, in the single case of Morès, from the archives of the North Dakota Historical Society. I am indebted to both institutions for permission to reproduce them, and especially to Mmes. Laurence Ratier and Jacqueline Sanson, conservateurs at the Bibliothèque, for their help in locating them.

Miriam Miller, editor of the Portable Stanford series, has my thanks for wielding her expert editorial pen on the manuscript. And I owe much to my wife, Louise A. Wright, for suggestions and encouragement.